BUSINESS IS PERSONAL

BE THE LEADER OF YOUR LIFE AND BUSINESS

Penny Power OBE

Business is Personal

First published in 2019 by

Panoma Press Ltd
48 St Vincent Drive, St Albans, Herts, AL1 5SJ, UK
info@panomapress.com
www.panomapress.com

Book layout by Neil Coe.

Printed on acid-free paper from managed forests.

ISBN 978-1-784521-52-3

The right of Penny Power OBE to be identified as the author of this work has been asserted in accordance with sections 77 and 78 of the Copyright, Designs and Patents Act 1988.

A CIP catalogue record for this book is available from the British Library.

This book is available online and in bookstores.

To my husband, Thomas, who always believed in me, even when I stopped. To Hannah, Ross and TJ who are now my mentors and inspire me daily. To all those who have given me lessons to learn. To all the friends, family and even strangers who gave me the courage to be unbroken and learn that I can make the choices I want in life, giving me the courage and skills to stand tall again as an entrepreneur and business owner.

TESTIMONIALS

"A whole manual for life in the modern workplace, how to live and how to work and how to be you. Penny nudges and nudges and has created a book that readers will return to for reminders and draw on for guidance during difficult moments in business. This is a brave book to write and an awesome book to read."

Don Tapscott CM, BA, BSc, MEd, LLD, CEO, The Tapscott Group Inc. / chancellor, Trent University / founder and executive chairman, Blockchain Research Institute, entrepreneur and co-author of *Blockchain Revolution: How the Technology Behind Bitcoin and other Cryptocurrencies is Changing the World*

"Being in business is about the ability to have a vision, to sell, to manage money, to attract caring people toward you and to have a determination to succeed. And yet, there is so much more to achieving business success, and this is where Penny's book comes into play. Penny highlights the essential emotional skills needed, and she does so with such open, heartfelt words regarding managing ourselves and being the leader of our own lives. This is a great read, essential in order to not only survive the modern business world, but to thrive and have fun along the way. Thank you, Penny, for showing us the way!"

Jack Daly, three-times #1 bestselling author and serial entrepreneur

"As a business owner, I face the daily challenges of the unknown and the extraordinary, many moments when I think I must be the only individually challenged business person when everyone else appears to be winning. Penny's book makes me feel normal, and that alone can be the catalyst to keep going."

Liz Harwood, owner, FAMARA Online

"Starting a business and looking after yourself is tough. With her wisdom and powerful personal stories, Penny shows you how."

Dr Ian Drever, MBChB, MRCPsych

"Having worked with Penny over recent years, I have come to know her well. Penny has a wisdom and desire for insight that has been a real pleasure to work with. She is blessed with great compassion and kindness – and a commitment to passing on the lessons she has learned."

Dr Anna Collins, chartered psychologist, The Psychology Clinic, Farnham

ACKNOWLEDGEMENTS

I would like to thank and acknowledge the following people for the incredible ways they have supported me on my journey of self-discovery, healing and learning. It is because of you that I have been able to write this book.

Thomas Power, my husband. Hannah Power, my daughter. TJ and Ross Power, my sons.

My incredible friends and extended family: my sisters Fiona Eastman and Dee Bromley, my dad Duff Ross. All my nieces and nephews, but particularly at this time, Rebecca Bromley and Alexander Eastman. My incredible business partner in The Business Café, Gail Thomas, my goodness her support has been relentless. My lifelong friends, Liz Harwood, Nicole Smart, Ailsa and William Adkin and Joan McCrossan.

To those who gave me advice and also through their actions, encouraged me to write this book. I have applied it all with such gratitude: Lis Cashin, Michelle Mackisack, Mindy Gibbins-Klein, Tracey Carr, Jane Swift, Dr Ian Drever, Anna Collins, Ruth Paris, David Cook, Merlie Calvert, Dale Clutterbuck, Richard Torble, Jacqui McGinn, Scott Keyser, Nicola Cairncross, Mary Haines, Cathy Richardson, Suzanne O'Callaghan, Anusha, Michelle Galbraith, Lenka Lutonska, James Knight, Alison Edgar, Hattie Hasan, Ronald Wopereis, Anita Brightley-Hodges, Simon Witts, Jay Shetty, Michelle Harris, Alison Raey-Jones, Walter Jennings, Chris Dudley, David Uffindell (vicar), Caroline Walker, Alex Birch, Tony Horan, Josh Williams, and Jamie Kemp.

The members of The Business Café Global Facebook community for all their incredible support, not only to me, but to each other.

To past and present business colleagues, Leon Benjamin, Glenn Watkins, Julian Bond, Andrew Widgery, William Buist, Anna Figiel, Daniel Priestley, Russell Butcher, Albert Wright, Helen

Richardson, Mark Estall, Adrian Grant, Bob Barker, Jonny Fry, Barbara Merry, Simon Esner, Russ Shaw, Amy Davidson, Jenna Owen, Tony Robinson OBE, Tina Boden, and Roger Hamilton, all especially mentioned in my book for the shared values we have and the way we supported dreams together.

This sounds a bit grand, but when you have read this you will understand – to the Queen and certain government employees who really believed in Ecademy and gave me so much confidence. I can't name you all, but thank you to Mark Prisk MP, Katherine Hathaway, and Rt Hon Anne Milton MP.

To people, some of whom have no idea who I am, but you inspired me during the tough times and on my writing journey and will do so beyond this point in my life: Nelson Mandela, Seth Godin, James Redfield, Katie Piper, Luke Johnson, Sir Tim Berners-Lee, Gary Chapman, Captain Charles Plumb, Ruby Wax, Gabby Bernstein, Don Tapscott, Jack Daly, Ed Molyneux, Gary Turner, Ronan Dunne, Robert Pickles, Richard Hanscott, Luke Johnson, Antony and Amanda Jenkins, and Alastair Stewart OBE.

CONTENTS

INTRODUCTION

This book is about you, what you want and what your personal desires are. It is written to speak to who you are and help you to be in control of your business and the desires you have for it. It is about helping you lead the life you want, not the life you think you should have.

What I have written in this book is personal and very open and honest. So many of us think that others sail through business, but the reality is that most of us have an unbelievable journey in order to learn the skills, mindset, and emotional management needed, as well as how to look after our souls and our physical health. The most valuable gift I can give you is to recognise that business is personal. I had to break in order to be whole, and I have learned so much through this process that is relevant to anyone hoping to avoid this and to those who are going through this experience themselves.

A number of months ago, I told my son Ross that I wanted to write a book that speaks to the person, not a book of systems or processes, but one about the whole person that we bring into business, the feelings we have and the torment that our emotions can put us through. I wanted people to know that it is normal to feel the way they do and to stop comparing themselves to others, believing everyone else has a better life.

A few days later, I bumped into a dear friend from my past called Scott Keyser. He told me that some words he had heard me say on stage several years ago had stayed with him. They were: "Business is personal".

I shared with my son that, thanks to Scott, I now had the title for my book. Ross went on to inspire me to create each chapter with the 'is Personal' as the focus. So here it is. Thanks to Ross, Scott and all the amazing people I have learned from, all mentioned within these pages. (I want to add that I was very tempted to call this book *Business is a Head F****). The words within will share both aspects, because it is personal and sometimes it does f*** with your head.

Why my book?

Starting out in business would have had different outcomes for me had I known what I know now. I don't mean the skills or the connections. I had not anticipated the emotional and mental challenges and the internal resources I would have to draw on. I did not anticipate the areas of my character and personality that would be tested.

I had the 'why', as Simon Sinek, author of *Start With Why,* calls it. Like many people, I knew my purpose. I had my passion and my core skills. I was missing the 'what': my understanding of what success, happiness and ambition was, along with what emotional, mental, spiritual and physical knowledge of myself I needed.

Twenty years on, I have discovered it is never too late. This book is for anyone starting out, or for those of us who have been battling on and would like to make the business journey match who we are and what we want out of life. Your business is personal to you. By the end of this book I want you to be able to stand up for the person you are in a complex, overwhelming and highly connected world, a confronting world that tests each of us daily. There is a way for you to feel more in control, a way to believe in yourself in a far deeper way than ever before.

There are many amazing writers on the subject of business, all seeking to provide the skills, mindset and inspiration for you to have a better business and be a better business person. I have been an avid follower and reader of all the people who could make me a better person. But what if you were already good enough and just needed to know your own path and believe in yourself more?

The danger of not knowing our own personal 'what' is that we can take on the expectations and dreams of others. In the world of social media and communication overload, we are confronted by the way others live their lives and run their businesses. The unsolicited advice, the feedback you come across online that knocks you sideways when you realise that, despite achieving in your own way, you are not doing enough or being enough. How long do we actually get to feel good and validated before we start to fight the inner voice that says: 'be more, do more'.

I call this book *Business is Personal* and I encourage you to discover your own 'what' in life. What makes you happy. What success means to you. What business relationships you want. What makes you feel in control and able to achieve the life you want.

To discover this, we need to explore our emotions, our mind, our soul and our respect for our physical health. We bring our whole selves into business, and that is what makes our business unique to each of us. That is also what makes us special to our clients and helps us to live our 'why' happily. It allows us to use our core skills with confidence, to deliver the business in a way that gives us peace of mind and the outcomes we want.

Starting out in business demands an incredible amount of courage and desire, as well as the skills we need to accumulate over time. We have our unique strengths that come naturally to us, but we also have to learn a layer above those that will turn us into the strong business people who can cope with adversity and rejection. We need to be able to manage the people we would not normally deal with and situations that cannot be anticipated.

It is the unknown that can impact our success. It is the way we emotionally handle things that can disrupt our future, the voices in our head, the lifetime of habits we discover have been hurting us and limiting our belief in ourselves. The outcome of all this encourages us to be like others, rather than be ourselves.

Accepting who I am, understanding what skills and attitudes I want and am willing to adopt, filtering out ideas and unsolicited advice, deciding on what happiness, success and business means to me personally – these are all turning points in my own peace of mind and joy of business ownership.

This book will take you on a journey to discover your 'what', because business is personal: it is your life, your business, your dream, your choice.

Let's go on the journey together so that you can shout: "Business is personal, and I love it."

CHAPTER 1

Business is Personal

I woke up with that dreaded feeling in my muscles and the anxiety in my chest. The words in my head circled: "why bother, who needs me anymore, I don't trust the outcomes, business is just too tough for me". And: "I am not one of those people who can make a business successful. I don't fit the profile of a rich, successful person".

The other words that struck me again, as they had so many times before: "business really can be a head f***" – and it is. There is no escaping that.

I still had that yearning, that desire, that need to be a business owner and fulfil the dream and purpose I had set out to achieve 19 years earlier. But, I finally realised I was a little bit broken, and I knew I had to go through a personal journey. I had been breaking for two years, maybe more, and I had finally acknowledged it and found enough courage to begin to learn more: more about myself and more about how to fit into this crazy world called business ownership.

Like you, I have loved my business life. From the very start I loved the independence, the daily passion I could apply to my work, the exhilaration of the growth in myself and my business and the feeling of achievement. I spent over 30 years in business with 20 of those years as a leader of my own business. I have been a small business owner and eventually an entrepreneur. I think big with my ideas because I like to solve big problems that are societal. I have launched two businesses that trailblazed new concepts, and I am now creating my third.

There are many of us who have decided on self-employment where the internet and the culture of economies have enabled us to start a business in a day. It is easy to get a bank account and quick to register a website. With the innate digital skills many have to use social media, we can begin to tell the world: "I am a business owner." It is truly fantastic.

Now in my 50s, having created some amazing businesses and stumbled many times, I want to see if my learning can help others. My journey has been a rocky one, and I called myself an accidental entrepreneur for years. Learning business as an owner, rather than working in a larger company, has tested me.

The aspects of business that have tested me most are the parts that do not come naturally to me. I have skills, I have drive and ambition. I can work hard and I can sell. I can build great teams and I can build a noise around me that gives my business the attention it needs. Where I fall down is due to the emotional and mental strength that is needed every day. I can have long periods of self-belief and resilience and then something builds up and I find myself anxious, stressed and out of control in my head. Like all startups, entrepreneurs and small business owners I know and have interviewed, I do a great job of hiding it. It is easy to hide the rapid heart rate, the sleepless nights and the stomach ache from fear. We can hide the confused minds and the searching for answers and trust.

The moment in my business life when a potential business partner said: "It's not personal, Penny, it's just business" was a truly defining moment in my business growth. The rage I felt, the trigger of 'how dare you' and the moment when I stood up for myself and said what I believed: "It is personal. What is more personal than the reason we get up, feed our families, spend our time and dedicate so much of our thinking to? Of course business is personal."

The internet is a great tool for us, it has changed the way business is done and opened up our worlds, made us more efficient and more connected. There is a 'but', and it is this: over the 20 years I spent supporting startups and small businesses, I witnessed enormous pressure from people comparing and striving based on other people's definitions of success and happiness. The open, transparent, online world that we live in has sucked us all into a whirlwind of other people's lives. It has created a sense of frustration, failure, guilt, regret and perfectionism that impacts our day-to-day emotional and mental state as we constantly strive for, and seek, the lives other people have, to be like them.

The statistics on business failures past one and five years are too depressing to discuss here. The reasons for them are varied. Financial concerns are always the main reason given – they ran out of money. However, I believe our emotional and mental strength governs our success. It is our ability to know ourselves deeply and to find the emotional strength to overcome the mental shocks and the real obstacles that inevitably come. *Business is Personal* is about nurturing your emotional and mental self, caring for your soul and being physically well enough to manage the roller-coaster. It is about having a mantra. Mine is: "Business is personal. It is mine and I am in control of what I want it to be and what it adds to my life and the lives of others."

When do you know that your business no longer feels personal to you?

The biggest factor in owning your own business is that you control the culture of your life, the hours and the business model. You are the leader of your dream. I have learned that we should look out for the moments when we let go of our instinctive knowledge and let go of what feels right. We should note those moments and trigger points when we have stopped being that leader, stopped being our own boss, stopped believing in ourselves and what we know – those are key moments.

Have any of those moments happened to you? Be aware of the moments in your future. These are the trigger moments: When someone else takes control of your business.

- When you find yourself acting like someone else.

- When you are affected by unsolicited advice.

- When you lose the passion you had because the business is starting to be something you don't want.

- When you make a decision that doesn't feel right to you.

- When you no longer have the strength to stand up for yourself.

- When you seek validation every day and know you have lost your inner belief.

- When you wake and no longer feel in control.

The truth is, we have all felt some of these at some point. Only you will know when this has taken hold of you. And when it does, you know what you need to do. You need to get your business back to the way you want it and make it personal to you.

Mindy Gibbins-Klein stated this beautifully in her book *The Thoughtful Leader*. We must: "Be careful about being influenced by others' thoughts and ideas. You will always be exposed to outside influences, but you don't have to be a pinball in a machine, being moved by external forces outside your control."

Holding on to your own beliefs and belief in yourself is the mindset of a strong entrepreneur. It is okay to ask for specific advice when you know exactly what you are seeking, and you can trust the knowledge and experience of your teacher. In this highly connected, open and overwhelming world of communication we are exposed to many thoughts and ideas. The best filters are your personal choices and desires. You know what you want and what is right for you.

Self-development or self-improvement

As a group, we spend millions on self-improvement books and courses to help us find our path to success. But, what if this book is different? This book is about you already being amazing and already having the ability to achieve the success you truly seek. The majority of people I have supported are already amazing, but they are so hard on themselves. The daily grind to be better has an impact on our emotional and mental states. I would like you to discover that you are already amazing, and to find a place within your soul that is kinder to yourself and allows space in your head to breathe and grow from within. To love yourself in business so that others can love you. To value yourself, so others can value you.

Overthinking – the plague of modern age

An online friend added to a thread I started on Facebook. I was asking people about the vast array of tests we can take online to analyse ourselves, to discover our strengths and weaknesses. I loved his reply:

"I think we are in danger of overanalysis of people, situations and ourselves. Not everything in life can be pigeonholed. Life is not perfect – we don't have weaknesses, we have characteristics. The real issue lies in how we find it necessary to stereotype and label everything. Be kind to others and generous in your thinking about yourself."

Stop comparing

We now live in a world where the temptation to compare ourselves with others, to be like elements of the people we see, is ever-present. We witness other people's lives and compare our happiness and success with what appears to be their perfect life. These thoughts are damaging and painful and impact the core of who we are and the life we could live if we focused on what is fulfilling and rewarding in our own lives. You cannot be that other person. Being you has to be enough, and it is. When I realised that, my life became whole.

Within these pages of thoughts, I have a dream for you: to be happy with who you are. When that happens you become more deeply connected with yourself, the people around you and with your business. The easiest person to be is yourself – no pretending, no acting. This is the real you that everyone wants to see and work with.

The take away I want you to have from this book is that your life is personal. It is your life. No one else's. No one should judge you – including yourself. The complexity of your life up to this point has made you the person you are. It has created your values, your ambitions, your view of what success is and your thoughts about what makes you happy. It has also created your pace, defined what you are willing to sacrifice and what aspects of life you will not let go of. It has given you skills, passion, meaning and purpose. Every day you have got up, applied your thoughts, beliefs and feelings to the day and then, at the end of the day, you got back into bed, sometimes satisfied with your achievements, sometimes lacking in joy, sometimes ecstatic with happiness.

Like our DNA, all the components of who and what we are, along with our thoughts, experiences and skills, are unique. How can we possibly compare ourselves to another person? It is for this reason that your life is personal, and so is your business. Your business IS personal to you.

Never feel small

> "If you think you are too small to make a difference, try sleeping with a mosquito."
>
> **Dalai Lama XIV**

Starting a business is the most courageous action anyone in the economy can take. From that point onwards, you are self-reliant. No salary will come in from anyone. I meet too many sole traders who say they feel small and irrelevant in the economy. You should never feel small when you have taken such a giant step. Every person I meet who owns a business makes me want to bow my head in respect for them and what they have done.

Arguably, a sole trader is the person I have the most pride in. Of course, getting to a point where you can employ others and support their families and dreams through your own endeavours of building a business is incredible. However, I rate the sole trader higher than others as they have many challenges and roles to play in their business. They often feel small and unimportant, and yet their skills are so diverse, as is their ability to drive themselves every day without accountability to others. They are amazing.

I have got used to being an entrepreneur

I was speaking to a new client recently and, in passing, he said: "I have got used to being an entrepreneur." I made a note of his words and later asked him what he meant. He struggled to define it but said it was a feeling, a mindset and an awareness of the ups and downs.

One constant among us all is that in choosing to be an entrepreneur we choose a life of ups and downs – a wave of highs and lows where the lows can be so low, and the highs can be so high. The drug of life is when all things come together. For that moment, that day, week or year, we are on top of the world. It is when our emotions and ambitions, our motivation, drive and our character all align. Those are the good days, and we seek those moments as entrepreneurs. We celebrate it when it happens, and we need to feel what happened, understand what made it happen and patiently wait for the next time. Because it will happen again.

We have to learn from the lows. A great gift in life is our self-awareness. The saying 'you learn more from how a person fights than how they love' is a great statement because you will learn more about yourself in the lows than you will when you are drinking the drug of success.

Never a victim, always the student

My take on this is that the strong, resilient entrepreneurs I know (the one I have been climbing back to be), are never a victim of the lessons they are forced to learn. This is one of the key things I want to help people achieve. Feeling let down, emotionally drained and lacking in self-belief are all components of an emotionally drained business owner. They are the words of someone who needs to step back and become strong again. When blame, anger, sadness and mental draining happens, this person needs to take tender loving care of themselves.

The aim is to get back to learning, to appreciating the moment of being a student again and deciding if this is a lesson you want to learn as you face the future with this newfound knowledge, or is this something you would never want to repeat? Remind yourself that business is personal, it is your choice, your business, your lesson.

Your personal lifeline

I was once asked by a wise business coach to draw a line from birth to death of the type of life I would like. Would it be a straight line with no ups and downs or would it have curves? The line I drew had quite large ups and downs. I felt it was the only way I would know I had truly lived. It may be worth thinking about this and being true to yourself.

Is it time we were all a bit more open?

Writing a book about the emotional and mental journey of business ownership would be pointless if I avoided the reality of the hard aspects of it. I have become tired and demotivated by the images of our mega entrepreneurs, the ones displayed on TV who treat entrepreneurs like idiots just because they don't know everything. I feel it is time for us all to be more honest about the journey and the realities. If each of us knew that others found it hard, there would be more respect, more love, and far more collaboration and trust in the ecosystem of business.

I have thought long and hard about this and decided now is the time to be real on paper and share my journey. At no time am I asking for pity – we all know that offers of sympathy are the most disempowering thing we can do for anyone. Acknowledgement of my strengths and weaknesses and my desire to fight back are the most I could ever seek. It was not easy to find my way back. As entrepreneurs, we hold ourselves up as resilient people but I lost my resilience. This book shows you the lessons I learned in my recovery and all the things I wish I had known about myself, and others, 20 years ago.

I feel if I can achieve just this message through my words, then I will have made a difference to you... If you imagine a line, above it is exceptional, below it is a feeling of being 'sub-standard', or 'below normal'. The line represents normal. To become exceptional we have to pass the line of normal. So many believe that they are lacking, that they are below normal. This makes it even harder to excel. I have spoken to so many thousands of people over my 20 years supporting business owners, and I know that emotions of fear, anxiety and low mood are normal, they are human. Challenges that hit us as business owners are also normal. We all learn and grow from them. I want you to know and feel that your emotions and your challenges are normal; once we all know this, then we can thrive, grow and become exceptional.

I have been fortunate to find a number of people who were also willing to share openly their stories and what they have learned, but I spoke to so many more. Believe me, as they say in America, being broken in business is a rite of passage, and it's time we all realised that those who have run a business, stumbled and got back up are amazing. If this is you, or if you are currently stumbling, I hope I can help you to stand tall again.

CHAPTER 2

Being Broken is Personal

"In Japan, broken objects are often repaired with gold. The flaw is seen as a unique piece of the object's history, which adds to its beauty. Consider this when you are broken."

This quote comes from the term Kintsugi, the art of precious scars. It is a true art form in Japan, based on the belief that it is possible to give a new lease of life to pottery that becomes even more refined thanks to its scars. It is possible to believe this is also true of human life.

We live in wonderful, enlightened times. There is definitely a rise in global consciousness. I first read about this in 1997 in *The Celestine Prophecy* by James Redfield. There is a belief that our minds are now evolving faster than our physical evolution, and we are becoming more connected, more open and more transparent. I have always been that way inclined: highly open with feelings and sensitive to those of others. For many years, I didn't feel like my values quite fitted the business world. Now, all around me, I see and feel similar values and many articles and Instagram posts showing how we are all part of this change.

Are we becoming more ORS?

In 2009 my husband, Thomas, articulated a deep belief he has held for many years. It is one that had been the heartbeat of the community we built together. He believed that the connected world was Open, Random and Supportive and the 'old world' in the pre-internet era of institutional thinking, was Closed, Selective and Controlling (CSC). We are in a period of total transparency and the desire for increased trust, which of course comes from honesty and openness and the demand for transparency that we see all around us.

It is strong to be vulnerable

Vulnerabilities are being seen as strengths if they are acknowledged and shared. From the CEO of a large company apologising with integrity rather than covering up issues, through to the forced openness through WikiLeaks and media exposure. Now we are asking for each of us to be real, even raw, and allow us all to connect with authenticity.

This means mental health and emotional wellbeing are being brought to the foreground of our lives. There are many amazing people who have stepped into the spotlight and declared their pains of bipolar disease, PTSD, anxiety and depression. They are inspiring the shift towards tolerance and kindness. All of this has a positive impact. The greatest of these is that we all start to feel more normal in our fears, pains and past experiences. The challenge is to ensure we don't create a nation or a world of victims. The true promise of this is that we create a stronger world, a world where people don't hide their pain and know that they can seek help.

Different levels of being open

I have never feared telling people face to face about my distress, my pains and my weaknesses. I think many friends and colleagues in the past would have called me far too open. Interestingly, I could retire on the number of people who have told me, as an English person, I would do well living in America. I am not sure what that says about the British mentality and culture, as opposed to the American one, but maybe it was the early access to therapists, or the limitations of the stiff upper lip, the traditional British way.

In being open, I thought I was dealing with my pain but the reverse was true. My openness was a comical mask, an act, a desire to cleanse through words. It took me 20 years to realise that healing can only be done quietly, calmly and with a great deal of thinking and discovery. Healing has to happen from the inside, from new discoveries of oneself and of the tools that can help. We have to be ready to listen and to heal.

My broken year

I went on a one-year journey to heal parts of myself and discover the skills from those around me in my community. By accident, a shock forced me to listen to myself. I am so grateful for that moment when my emotional, mental, spiritual and physical being said 'stop'. It was time I looked after myself.

To this day, I am not sure if this was burnout, a mini-breakdown or a warning. I never stopped functioning. I continued to work, but at a different pace. The biggest transformation was that I asked for help. My name for those who helped me are my Earth Angels – you can call them your mentors or your friends. As I say later in the book: "These people have packed my parachute." My Earth Angels are talented business people whom I could relate to and who had insights from their own life experiences and from studying their subjects deeply. In some instances I had known them for years, but I had not truly understood the depth of their skills until I was ready to tune in.

While I was on my own discovery of the things I wish I had been aware of 20 years ago, I kept noting my lessons. I knew I would write this book one day, because I knew that much of what I was going through was more common than any of us like to admit.

Twenty years to tune in and realise I was hiding my pain behind my life purpose

The saying 'physician heal thyself' is a powerful term. I have always loved to give kindness, to help people be themselves and to love themselves. It is often true that we build our own businesses from a place of personal adversity. Using our own knowledge and personal limitations gives us the empathy and desire to help others.

In 2005, over a relaxing drink at a conference I was speaking at in Bali, a fellow speaker said: "Penny, you are un-coachable." I was immediately offended for some reason and my defences went up and stupidly I never asked him what he meant. Thirteen years later, I think I got what he was trying to tell me: I was too independent to allow anyone to help me. Why? Because it was much easier to deflect the attention away and help others.

This is a trait common to many of the people I studied when I was researching loneliness, studying this helped me to understand what my type of loneliness was too. I wasn't lonely in a friend or family way, I was deeply lonely in business. I had no sense of belonging. When I took time to reflect, I realised that the healing I wanted to give others by creating communities and writing about the importance of deep connections was actually the very thing I needed. It was easier to hide my needs behind my purpose.

Being unable to ask for help or trust others to have good intentions, and know that they would like to help, has been a very enlightening journey for me. I don't want to go into the childhood reasons I must have learned this pattern of behaviour, as it would not serve you for me to do that, nor would it serve my memories of childhood. Some of the loneliest people I interviewed were the most independent. I suggest that you will be driven by your own adversities, unknowingly healing yourself through the healing of others. This makes it very real and provides deep levels of empathy. However, as the saying goes, 'pouring from an empty vessel' cannot be sustained. We have to ensure our own cup overflows before we can really help others.

Being broken becomes your strength

"To become whole, first let yourself be broken."

Lau Tzu

Your life will be defined by all the things you have absorbed, hidden, dealt with and drawn on. These things will have formed your thoughts, beliefs and feelings about yourself. I am hoping the majority of this is positive and your life has been great. It is normal to have times of adversity as well as the voice in our heads that we try to reconcile. If we could hear the internal thoughts of those key people we have known, (even those who display great success and joy), we would hear the same sounds of anxiety, pain, frustration, anger, loss and fear as we would throughout the global population and throughout eternity.

Last year I read a book about the Psalms (written before Christ, over 2,000 years ago) and the emotional and mental needs were exactly as ours are now. We might progress technologically, and humanity might not be as barbaric as they were in the times of the Gladiators, but the human needs are the same now as they were then.

The emotional needs remain the same. We need love and connection, safety, certainty, belonging and self-esteem. We need to feel significant and to contribute in a meaningful way. We need personal growth, variety and challenge. This is well documented and was formulated famously by Abraham Maslow in his 1943 paper which included the Hierarchy of Needs.

We should enjoy the journey of self-discovery and self-improvement, but "stay hungry and stay foolish" as the great Steve Jobs said in his 2005 Stanford speech. Work in progress is very motivating.

My story of being broken

Indulging in writing about myself has taken many edits. Each time I have shown my words to those who have been on a journey, they have said: "You are still hiding." I think my fear of sharing is that I don't want to overindulge in my own story. However, I think different aspects of it will resonate with different people. Additionally, there is a history behind this, of the emerging socially connected world that is like a timeline. To some this may also fascinate. I hope it will also provide the context to understand my loss and my reason for breaking.

Let me start by saying that my core personality is happy. I love people, I love life. I am a positive person – I like to laugh and I like to make others laugh. I need to contribute to others. I am a patient person and I am giving by nature. I am a people pleaser. All these in balance are okay. I am not the cleverest, funniest person I know, but I tick along and have achieved an average life in education and career.

I was told by a psychologist that I am very typical of the type of person Dr Tim Cantopher writes about in his book *The Curse of the*

Strong. The type who is susceptible to a kind of depression unique in its appearance as the person never gives up, never shows signs of depression until one day… they break.

Some background to who I am

I joined the IT industry in 1983 when I was 19, reluctantly, having got a place at university to study psychology and then financially being unable to take the place up. Happily, my son TJ, aged 21 as I write this, is studying Psychology at Exeter University, so while we cannot live our lives through our children, I feel some of my DNA is enjoying this. I started in telesales and over a 10-year career I worked for four different companies and completed my employed life as a Sales and Marketing Director with around 300 staff and an £80m revenue. This was a good company in the 1980s, selling the major hardware and software brands of its time.

When I gave birth to our first baby, Hannah, in 1992, I stopped working, which was a huge planned adjustment. At 28, Thomas became a father and the sole breadwinner. We lived a modest life in a small semi-detached Victorian house in Farnham, Surrey. Money was tight and I worked for three years in a self-employed and very erratic way doing various things from selling baby equipment to recruitment.

I gave birth to Ross in 1994, and it was around this time that I started to support a man who left Dell to create a network of home-based computer sales people, selling home PCs. It was an exciting business. In 1995, home computing was emerging and the channels to buy were not like they are now. I built a network of 650 agents, wrote training manuals, ran events and trained new agents on a Saturday while Thomas looked after our two, soon to be three, children. The business was massively disrupted when PC World took hold in the High Street. The founders decided to move the operation to America. Moving to America was not an option for us, we were happy in the UK and was also timed with the birth of my third child, our son TJ.

I was not extraordinary. I worked hard. I communicated well, and I built trust in people. I supported the network of agents I had built via email. Social networking did yet exist. By then, Thomas and I had moved to a larger house – he was doing very well in his business and life was good. Thomas was consulting and speaking on e-commerce and would teach me about this new internet world that was a far cry from my previous life of processes and skills.

My ah-ha moment

In February 1998, we were sitting in Pizza Express in Farnham with our three children when I shared a vision with Thomas of an online community for self-employed people, or those with small businesses. Thomas is an awesome networker, and he was struggling with the demands of his business to manage the delivery and achieve the joy he got from networking and connecting people. I talked about a global, online community where people could connect with one another rather than rely on him to be the connector.

Ecademy was born

Thomas loved my idea. Very early on in my planning for Ecademy, I met a man who had sold his IT business to a client of mine, who also loved the idea and invested £250,000. He took on the role of CEO as the role was not right for either of us. Thomas's skills were to build the community, speak and sell, while mine were to manage the culture of the platform and build the community from the inside once people had joined.

Over the years this grew and grew into something quite amazing. We welcomed all new members, understood their needs and desires and when Glenn Watkins and Julian Bond became Directors in 2002, we added blogging, the ability to add your own events, plus the ability to have your own 'group'. This was all before LinkedIn and Facebook. We were educating the market and charging £10 a month subscription. We invested hard into the business and took a small salary from it. We soon realised we had given birth to something quite amazing in both its impact and the life it could potentially give us.

In 2000 we were in the media a lot. The assumption was that we were one of the dotcom millionaires who were springing up like rabbits. The sudden rise in 'perceived fortune', and the pressures that accompany this cannot be underestimated.

Accidental entrepreneur

I am an accidental entrepreneur, not naturally able to cope with the financial risks and the hard knocks of business. Emotionally, this period stretched me: the financial risk, the juggle of motherhood, the travel that Thomas did all over the world while I stayed at home to be with the children.

Aged 35, Thomas and I were valued on paper at £22m with an IPO planned for 18 March 2000. This cost us a vast amount of money, and in preparing we had taken on 40 shareholders and financial commitments to scale the business. Two of our investors were family and two were friends. They say 'friends and family first' when seeking investment. I now say that is the best way to completely destroy your life.

If you Google 'the dotcom crash' you will read that the market peaked on 10 March 2000 and then crashed. At the beginning of March, we were highly exposed, and our nominated advisers provided constant updates on where we were in the queue – the queue for the bell to ring at the AIM Stock Exchange. Then we got the call – the crash had happened, lastminute.com were the last to go, and ours was cancelled.

When the first rug gets pulled

That was the first of many pains. The first cut is the deepest I guess. The wonderful truth is that you become more resilient with each cut. The wonderful term 'this is the new norm' helps a great deal. You have to get used to the new norm, but let's not underestimate the depth of these cuts and the pain that lies beneath the scars. On a practical level, our first investor took this pretty hard. He had also nominated himself as the CEO and he felt the pressure deeply. Thomas and I were so committed to the purpose of the business and our founding beliefs that we never questioned carrying on. Cash was tight, people were laid off, the office closed in London and we returned home to work and maintain the asset we were building – our community of business owners.

Then we were fired

The summer of 2000, three months after our withdrawn IPO, Thomas and I were summoned to a hotel in Slough by our CEO and an investor. It was the day of our son Ross's Sports Day and I was hesitant to go. We negotiated the timing to ensure I would be at his school in time. Arriving at the hotel, we knew something wasn't right. We were presented with paperwork and forced to resign. Our shares could not equal the voting rights of our CEO and the investors he had corralled. We took it on the nose. Their belief was that Ecademy should become an e-learning portal and, as our skills, passion and belief were about communities for business, they said we were no longer required.

As a mum, my only thoughts were to get out of there and ensure I could watch my son run. We dashed out of the hotel, confronted the most almighty traffic jam on the M25 caused by sheep on the road, drove down the inside lane, and arrived two hours later at our son's playground in time for me to join the Mums' Race. All I needed was my son's beautiful smile and I forgot all about the future we needed to protect.

We all just carried on

At that time, we were building the membership of Ecademy. Our CTO was Glenn Watkins and thankfully we were not removed from using the platform. We contacted Glenn, whom I had worked with when I was building the Home Computing Network, and advised him that while we would continue to work on the business, we were no longer executives of the company. Our CEO was happy for us to volunteer our time, and we were discreet and kept the issues of our Board to ourselves. Key staff were not being paid by the business but were critical to its survival, and so we began to take out personal loans so we could pay them privately, directly, to keep them inside and progressing the business.

We got Ecademy back

Thomas and I continued to meet members and go to the fabulous meetups we had started having in 1999. Ecademy was about the online and the offline. This status quo continued until in April 2002 when the CEO of Ecademy met with Thomas and put an offer on the table for us to buy his shares back and take back control of Ecademy. This was more debt for us. However, our belief in business communities continued and we could see the growth in our membership – we never stopped believing.

Our first competitor came to market

Thomas was travelling the world by now, visiting our members. In late 2002, Glenn became our CEO and recruited our amazing CTO, Julian Bond, who had been a supplier under our previous CEO's reign. They were amazing to work with.

Thomas was the case study and constantly asked for more and more code. We brought to market the ability to blog in a community, create your own groups and place events in our event calendar. Our members loved it. They were building global relationships, travelling to see each other and running local events through the groups and event calendar. We were running training sessions and creating IP around how to build your online brand. Andrew Widgery joined us on the journey of building the local groups and was an incredible asset to the growth and culture of Ecademy. To this day, Andrew remains a wonderful friend and believer in connecting and supporting business people.

Thomas was highly engaged with our members, one of whom was Reid Hoffman. On 5 May 2003, LinkedIn launched, having been founded as a Business Network in December 2002 by none other than Reid Hoffman himself. Ecademy was no longer alone in the market.

We embraced our competitors

Thomas and I firmly believe that any business has to exist for the good of its customers. LinkedIn was a powerful platform and our members were curious. Thomas talked about the importance of being on all networks when he did his public speaking events and shared thoughts on our blogs. When LinkedIn launched it had an invitation system – a brilliant idea of theirs. Thomas joined LinkedIn in 2003, a couple of months after it launched, and using the invitation system he sent an email to our 10,000 members inviting them to join his network on LinkedIn and 5–10% joined. They discussed this a great deal on our blogs and thanked Thomas for always looking after their needs.

Happy times

We carried on growing and building a powerful global network. At its peak, we had 650,000 members with 25,000 paying a subscription in 2005. Subscriptions were rare at that time and selling Software as a Service (now SaaS) had not yet been created. Thomas and I juggled family life together. Our whole priority in life has been our three children, all at private schools by now, our life was extremely busy and had many classic business ups and downs.

Between 2002 and 2005 we were managing. Facebook launched in 2004 and had no effect on us as they were focused on students and young people at the time. I remember chairing the first (known) social media conference in 2007 and was on the stage with Facebook and LinkedIn. They both defended their positions, one in the business sector the other in the social space. I felt safe. Ecademy was a hybrid and helped business owners become friends, so it was a cross between the two.

How much will you sacrifice?

In 2007, we saw a steady decline in new members as we started to defend our space. LinkedIn were offering many of the tools we charged for, but theirs were free. Some members started to become edgy with us. We had experienced trolls from 2005 but the rise in people questioning our business model and telling us how to run the business grew.

The amount of unsolicited advice people give always fascinates me. This is something of a challenge for all scalable business owners, those who feel they know better than you. The user experience is critical to any software company; however, you have to learn to filter and manage the business with all the facts you have at your disposal. We unofficially called these people the 'what you need to do club'. We started to reinvest into the business by reducing and then stopping our personal income. Thomas predicted a decline in the housing market, and in July 2007 we sold our house and moved into a rental property. We had re-mortgaged enough and any decline in our house price would have saddled us with a huge level of debt.

I still have a picture of our children all bundled into the back of our estate car, teddies and critical personal belongings around them. Aged 15, 13 and 10 they were adaptable, but they weren't ignorant to the fact that we were suffering financially. All three children had travelled with us to Asia, Holland, Denmark and America to meet members where they were equipped with name badges and handshakes. They already knew the game and understood how much Ecademy meant to us all as a family. Ecademy was our business family. To this day they have so many members of ours as connections on Facebook, Twitter and LinkedIn. They all laugh at the occasional comment or message they get from people who feel they know them so well. Thomas and I appreciate this so much.

The bank loan

In 2008, we knew we had to change our business model and open our community to members for free. The disruption caused by the world of 'free' was not only impacting us, it was impacting many business models. Some call this progress – I call it devastation. The impact on small businesses was enormous. Access to knowledge had been devalued, which I write about later. However, what really hurt was our belief system that people were able to verify their true identity through their bank details. 'Free' opened the world to the anonymous, the trolls and the hatred that we now see taking away the promise of a beautifully connected world.

For us to survive though, we had to grow our member base and move over to the advertising models. The brands were not interested in levels of engagement or the stickiness of your community, nor the culture or ethics we believed in. The agents they used to place adverts only wanted clicks. This was a volume game.

In April 2008, we borrowed £250,000 and set about re-energising and reconfiguring our community. Code had to be written, brands had to be sold to. We had to become different beasts as a Board, and we were now in survival mode. Our closest members were, and remain, our closest advocates and friends. Thankfully, in November 2004, Thomas had launched Blackstar, a premium membership. Thomas and I could maintain the intimacy we believed in with this group, and their higher fees helped us to keep the business afloat.

Another two offers to save our bacon

During the final years of Ecademy, we had two further offers for the business. One was a trade sale that would enable Thomas and I to keep the community going – it was from a German network, but we rejected it after a lot of negotiation as it was a share swap. They also admitted their plan was to close Ecademy to remove us as an irritant in the market. The second, and truly exciting one, was from a major High Street bank in May 2011. This got all the way to the final champagne moment of signing. But, on that day, their group CEO was exposed – the banking crisis was in full swing, and the offer was retracted face to face in their grand offices, two hours into me chilling the champagne with Glenn's wife and my colleague, Sophia. We had been dealt another blow. Again, out of our control.

The cuts reopen wounds and go deeper

Each business challenge knocks you, but it is the time it takes to recover that matters. This is the kind of resilience we all need – that ability to bounce back. Much like your heart after exercise, you seek to return to a steady pace as fast as you can. How you do this is a skill. For me, it was about focusing on my deep purpose, gratitude for my marriage and my children, and hope. The belief that eventually all will be great.

The final blow

In September 2011, deep within the banking crisis, our loan bank issued a demand for our final debt to be paid back within 30 days, two years before it was due. That letter was our final and deepest cut. We had managed so much: cancelled IPOs, being fired, offers being retracted, losing our home, trolls, massive personal debt and sleepless nights that became the norm. Our tenacity and resilience and health were being tested for a final time. Glenn had resigned after the bank offer had been retracted and we had amicably parted company.

Thomas and I were on our knees and we spent 27 days knocking on doors hoping for a rich investor or organisation to buy our business and give us some hope. The market was flooded with people who were buying distressed companies. This became our only hope. We had nothing left.

On 20 July 2011, Ecademy was sold. The bank had won.

Do we always manage things the way we hope?

The confidential nature of what was happening, the legalities and the sheer exhaustion and grief we felt meant we couldn't communicate with all those we wanted to about what was going on. The new owner allowed me to post a final blog – the words of which I still hold on my hard drive. I am never sure how many people read it.

Let's not forget, for all of us who have lost a business, there is a grief and a deep sadness. All the hopes and dreams, all the work, all the love you poured into it has gone. I often think about the assets our members lost: their content, their connections and their business home.

The emotional impact

The impact on us was enormous. In 2011, Thomas and I were broken, not only financially, but mentally. Our self-esteem and self-belief were gone, along with our community, which was like our extended family. We were reduced to scarcity and had to find a way to come back. Like coming out of a painful marriage and then considering marrying again, it takes time to trust. We needed time to build our strength and belief in not only ourselves, but in others. Inevitably, anyone who has been at the top of their game discovers the people they can still trust and those who were just there for the ride.

You can't give up, you have to keep earning

During the period when we were trying to save our sinking ship, I wrote my first book, *Know Me, Like Me, Follow Me* published in 2009. At the time there were very few books on how to build communities and your brand. This coincided with a new prime minister and a new attitude.

Small businesses and entrepreneurship were the latest buzzwords in government, and I was asked to come in and advise on how they could support small businesses. Their plan, due to the large national debt in the UK, was to close Business Link and the Regional Development Agencies in the UK. It seemed a weird decision when they knew the economy needed innovation and entrepreneurship to rebuild from the recession. However, the decision was made. I banged the drum for digital skills for all as everyone needed to understand the importance that digital held for all businesses, not just within the tech sector, or the newly named digital sector.

I wrote the manifesto for Digital Business Britain and from this came my second business: the Digital Youth Academy. I secured investment from a lady who had an OBE from her work in the youth sector and, together with an amazing team of people, we created the first Digital Marketing Apprenticeship. By working with further education colleges and authorised training providers, we helped over 1,000 young unemployed people into work, also achieving my plan to help small businesses 'go digital'. I loved the business. I also loved that it opened up a new set of skills for me – I had an understanding of the skills sector, how it worked and how it was funded.

Digital Youth Academy ran its course and the sector became saturated as we were no longer the only supplier of this skill. City and Guilds entered the market and I am thrilled to say the digital marketing apprenticeship we founded and trailblazed soon became a normal apprenticeship for all young people and those wanting to reskill. My investors and I chose to sell it, relatively successfully, to a national training provider.

A light in all the darkness, the power of validation

I worked like crazy during the period from the loss of Ecademy through to 2015 – those were four very tough years. I was running on empty, working 16 hours a day, using up huge amounts of mental energy, travelling the UK to speak and evangelise our business of helping youths. In November 2013, I received a letter awarding me an OBE for 'Ecademy and our Contribution to Entrepreneurship in the Social Digital Economy' – it was a spark of utter joy. The shock of this was enormous and its impact was life changing for me. I had a warmth inside me that I will never lose. At last we had been recognised for what we had done. Ecademy was no longer part of our lives, but what we had done had been acknowledged at the highest possible level.

The impact of awards and the recognition they bring cannot be underestimated. The validation and sense of self-worth was priceless. The Queen 'had packed my parachute', (you will understand this statement later in the book).

My amazing man

While I am sharing my story here, I cannot ignore the role Thomas has played. His pain was greater than mine as he had put an enormous amount of work into Ecademy – far greater than I had. His impact on people was incredible and my pride in him grows every day through his constant determination and generosity, and the positivity he shows in his every breath and being. I believe the OBE was a shared honour, but he never allowed it to be. That is the man he is. Thomas has never allowed himself to be broken, not outwardly at any rate. He has maintained our income and been the bravest person I know. He stayed positive, loving, patient and giving and is my ultimate inspiration on how to be an entrepreneur.

Knowing you are no longer broken

It is important to teach and share in a way that gives hope. I hope that by sharing my journey you can pinpoint the things you might have done – we can all act as great sounding boards. It is also important to share the moment when you know you are no longer broken. The wave of self-esteem and self-worth that comes back means you can stand tall again, stand up for what is right and return to the person fuelled with self-belief and a passion to continue your quest. This is when you are no longer daunted or fearful of the rejection of others, you are no longer defensive or overcompensating for your broken spirit. Now you are able to rebuild with the energy, confidence and the lessons from the past that used to fill you with self-loathing.

Getting past problems makes you happy

"Don't wait for the storm to pass, learn to dance in the rain."

Anon

I talk later about happiness – a desire we all have. I have learned that happiness goes in waves. In business we must accept that there will be few moments of calm and predictability. Our happiness can be taken away in an email, a meeting or in a moment. A shock will come, and you feel the drain of energy and happiness leaving you. I now embrace these moments and look forward to happiness. The happiness returns as soon as you move forward and solve a problem. Pride in yourself creates happiness. Knowing each time that you overcame the blip, you rise above the challenge. That is business happiness.

Stress is personal, your personal head f***

Stress is the aspect of business we all seek to avoid. It is physical, and you will feel it in your heart, your stomach, even in your muscles. Later, in the chapter Physical Wellbeing is Personal, I share the chemical reaction that happens.

It is important to know that some stress is good stress. I also know that we have to accept it as part of life. We all react differently – stress is personal. I know I react in a different way from Thomas. We both respect and give space to the way we deal with stress. For me, shock and change will impact me for about three days. I can timeline it and know that I will get used to the new norm, and I will accept it as part of life, because that is exactly what it is.

When a blow comes, I retreat for a day, go quiet, allow myself to be frustrated. I call this period a Head F***, which Thomas and I always laugh about. Business plays with your head. Just when you feel you are coasting along, it will tell you to get back into the stormy waters. On that day, I know I need to put on my life jacket and ensure I have the strength in my mind and body to navigate what is to come. When I wake the next day, I am ready to sail again. What I love about the stormy waters is that I am at my best: I am creative, I am strong and I am powerful. I find an inner positivity that shocks me. Nothing will break me again – I know what that feels like.

Then happiness returns as I am back at the top of a wave with oxygen to breathe. I see a horizon and I'm finding a way to reach it again.

Starting again, with new self-awareness

In 2014, while in the midst of this chaos, I sat in a coffee shop in Farnham feeling deeply alone but surrounded by people. Many of us had laptops open and were clearly local business people. I decided to try and speak to the person next to me. I failed to engage and was given a short, brisk reply. Embarrassed and uneasy from this, I started to close my laptop when my inner voice said: wouldn't it be amazing if there was a coffee shop just for business people? A business café, with a culture of love and inclusion and friendship, not a co-working space, but a social space to relax, be friends and help one another – the same cultural intent as we fostered at Ecademy. I felt inspired and wrote two pages of what it would be like and blogged this on 27 October 2014. I gave birth there and then to my third business.

Taking responsibility for my past and moving on

Self-awareness once again becomes important before you can move forward in a stronger and more positive way. I want to make a dent and have an impact, and the world I care deeply about is that of the small business, the sole trader, the startup. The two businesses under my belt have achieved some amazing things, but the strain on me, and the feeling that I had not completed the full vision I held for them, made me cautious of my emotional and mental stamina, as well as my skills.

There were parts of me that had to heal, parts of me that had to be stronger, parts of me that had to accept the past. I had to take responsibility for the reasons neither of my businesses achieved the long-lasting impact and financial returns they both deserved.

To fully extract myself from the chaotic business structures and relationships I had created since the sale of Ecademy, I had to start afresh. I had to find a symbolic way to say one part of my life was over and another was starting. I bought a helium balloon and wrote down some words of pain on a piece of paper and words of hope on another. I went out into the garden and made a small fire from the words of pain and attached my words of hope to the balloon. I cried tears of joy as I watched the balloon fly high with the words The Business Café attached. I cried with relief when I saw the pain-filled paper of names turn to ash.

Symbolism is important for starting to achieve closure and for new beginnings.

It takes time

Coming back from being broken is not about time, or a stiff upper lip, nor is it about boxing it up, burning it or pretending it doesn't matter. I truly believe when you dismiss pain and pretend it doesn't matter, it will end up being everything. Deep, chronic pain can be too easily ignored. We have learned to live with it and accept that state of mind as the norm. But we should not put up with it, whether emotional, mental, spiritual, physical or financial. None of these can be endured endlessly. No matter how long it takes, and for me it took years, the pain eventually surfaces and we learn the reasons we may have limited our lives. Fear, anger, trust and personal characteristics will all have played a part, and we have to unpack them all and enjoy the new discoveries.

Phrases like 'this too will pass' are wonderful – it is true, stressful times will pass. But when you find yourself repeating the same mistakes, creating the same outcomes, then you know that something deeper has to happen to change your future and allow the life you want to show itself.

'The struggle is my life' – is this the mantra for all entrepreneurs?

Nelson Mandela once said: "The struggle is my life." For some reason I have always loved that statement. He was a man who knew and accepted that in order for change to happen he had to accept the struggle. I love to work towards something, because I often think that the only animals to get their food given to them (apart from dogs and cats in happy homes) are those in cages. The rest of the animal kingdom has to struggle to find food, shelter, safety, and even a position in their own tribes. That is what freedom is – the freedom to choose how we live our lives. Freedom comes with the costs of hunting for food. It is freedom that often motivates people to leave companies and start their own business.

I believe we should never confuse freedom with a full tummy. The decision to work for yourself means you will always strive for something more. Strife can be positive, as long as the strife you have is linked to a purpose, and as long as it is at a level that won't emotionally or mentally impact you.

My own healing began on 30 November 2017 after a health warning in the form of exhaustion and hallucinations. I had been dealing with my business pain as well as all the inevitable family pain from the last four years: the sudden death of my beautiful niece at the age of 29 – she died of cancer in January 2014; I lost my brother to pancreatic cancer in 2016; my mother declined through dementia from 2010 and passed away in 2017; and my amazing daughter suffered a massive trauma. All have taken their toll on me.

Opening the drawer and shoving it in

I had perfected my stress: I took it all on the nose, opened a metaphorical drawer and shoved my pain inside. The rest of this book is dedicated to all those who may do the same. It is common because we fear the pain of considering our losses and their impact. We are told over and over again to be positive, strong, and to let go. We focus on caring for others and helping them, but it doesn't work. We have to commit to feeling our pain and accepting it. We have to commit to understanding the lessons we have learned, and how to grow from them. Placing our emotions in drawers and saying "they have gone away now" does not work. You do not grow and it doesn't heal the pain below the scars.

Three amazing people share their learnings of being broken

Every story of adversity and of being broken has its lessons. The following stories will give you an element of the broken times along with the great lessons we can each learn. If you can read these experiences with the intent to learn and avoid, then we have all done a great service to the startup and entrepreneurial world.

Tracey Carr - building goalshaper.com "my shareholder experience"

Tracey and I are connected on Facebook and have met for coffee a number of times to share experiences and advice. She is an entrepreneur through and through and she wants to create a scale-up business, and to support others. She is brilliant at networking and partnerships and has a strong passion for coaching and helping people to define and achieve their goals. Her digital platform www.goalshaper.com is being used by partnership companies and directly by clients.

Tracey openly admits to having been broken in business. Her spirit was broken and she lost all confidence in herself. Her feeling of being kicked in the stomach manifested itself as bruises on her stomach – an interesting aspect of the link between our mental and physical being, which I cover in Chapter 9.

A challenging shareholder

Tracey's lesson in business came from the experience of taking on an investor who turned into an online abuser and personally attacked Tracey's integrity. When I interviewed her for this book, it was amazing to hear the tone in her voice, the survival, growth and acknowledgement of her part in this – another true mark of an entrepreneur. Tracey stated that it took time to get to this place: "when you are in the pain of a situation it is hard to see the lessons in life. Survival is your highest priority when being attacked in business, in whatever way you are receiving it".

Tracey shared that her greatest lesson came from her fear of conflict and her previous inability to confront situations and nip things in the bud. I think this is very common. It is hard when people question and show anger. Our easiest path is to defend and avoid. We are so busy, we just want to get rid of the person and the issue. The courage, patience and objectivity we need when dealing with someone who has begun to attack is immense. Of course, we would all like to behave in a perfect manner, but we are not perfect. It is our imperfections that makes us human.

We often read anger and feel attacked by people when they are actually acting from fear and their own vulnerabilities. Tracey knows now that had she managed the situation better at the beginning, things would have been calmer. We never know if this is the case. Some people are just hell-bent on causing harm. I think Tracey is hard on herself, but her lesson to us all is one I am grateful for.

Tracey's turning point

To recover, Tracey took one small step each day in rebuilding herself and her business. She said she felt physically weak and had to manage the energy she had carefully. On a practical level, in order to regain control, Tracey asked the police for help, and a Harassment Warning Notice was issued to the individual. Then she focused on surrounding herself with people who believed in her as a person, not just in her business. We have to counter negative energy with good energy – a really sound plan for all of us when we are drowning in a negative situation. The result of her new focus on people was that many of her business friends decided to invest in her.

Tracey also learned that she must trust her intuition. She could have avoided the pain had she realised from the start that this investor wasn't the right person to have around her business (a lesson I learned the hard way, twice). Sometimes we just see the money as a solution and don't realise we are only solving a short-term issue and creating a long-term problem.

Bob Smith (using a pseudonym) – starting a business with the wrong business partner

A member of a community I belong to offered me their story. Bob's story is highly relevant because it's about being broken in work and marriage by starting a business with his wife. This is a heartbreaking story because it was avoidable.

Bob and his wife had a good marriage, they both had jobs and an average level of ambition. Their life was steady if a bit predictable for Bob. A couple of years into marriage and with a young son, Bob suggested to his wife that they started their own business. His wife took a lot of persuading and eventually agreed. In hindsight, Bob feels she did this to make him happy rather than buying into the life of an entrepreneur. It never went well according to Bob. Every day was a struggle as his wife showed huge signs of stress around money, frightened to invest in any marketing or business promotion and tying Bob's hands (metaphorically). They argued constantly and shared endless frustrations. Eventually, his wife left.

I understand this issue because some of us are prone to risk aversion and some of us can cope with the uncertainty of money. Thomas and I had the same challenges, but we both believed in the purpose and mission of the business.

Bob said the underlying feeling in their daily lives was one of negativity where nothing was ever enough, where no win could be celebrated as it couldn't counter the risk his wife felt they were taking. She stopped contributing, saying it was too hard. It could be that his wife was bordering on depression, which has a measureable impact on clarity and energy.

No one is at fault

Bob and I talked at length about the lessons to be learned from this experience. The most critical point centred around who you choose to go into business with. That person needs to be upfront about their expectations, outcomes, feelings and desires. Too many businesses fall apart due to a conflict between the business partners. Starting a business has to begin with honest and truthful communication.

Bob's turning point

Sad as it is, Bob's turning point came when he was able to build the business with the energy and clarity of working on it alone. Saving his marriage wasn't possible, but ensuring that a business could rise up and support his son and enable him to achieve his newfound ambitions was critical. You cannot sink, you have to find a way forward. I think Bob is recovering from his loss – there is no anger, just a sadness over what could have been avoided.

Sarah Shaw (pseudonym) – discovers her future from being broken

Sarah never imagined herself being self-employed – she was an employee with little ambition for herself. The ultimate goal for Sarah was to get married and have children. These smaller dreams in her business career were brought on by her life partner who was successful and liked her to be at home, supporting him. During this time Sarah's father died and losing him gave her the first emotional crisis in her life.

Being broken

Sarah became depressed and intimidated and leaned more and more on her life partner. One day her best friend suggested that her issue was actually that she was living with a narcissist. Desperate to cling to a reason and find blame, Sarah believed this and moved out. She then drowned herself in self-hatred and lost trust in people and herself. During this time she travelled alone and it was while travelling that Sarah decided to start her own business while working as a part-time teacher.

What business could I start?

Knowing that she had a desire to own a business, Sarah started to look for signs of what type of business she could start and noticed that she was seeing signs of herself in others. She could feel the pain that others were in and through informal coaching she was making a difference to them. Sarah knew she needed to become qualified and gain the skills to effectively coach others.

Breakthrough moment

Like many self-employed people, they begin a business with a purpose, with the innate skills to help others, or deliver a product or service. The one thing that can hold them back are the business skills. Attending a business boot camp with her purpose firmly understood enabled Sarah to gain the skills she needed to become a business person. She gained insights into how to connect herself with her new persona by understanding what she was here to do and being able to frame her life experiences as great learning that now floods her mind and soul with purpose.

Sarah says she is grateful for the moment she broke. The quote from Lau Tzu at the start of this section is so true for Sarah: "To become whole, first let yourself be broken."

Hope

Before I take you to all the ways I have learned to be an emotionally and mentally stronger person in business, let me share one last quote in this chapter that left me in tears. This was stated by Katie Piper, a remarkable lady, who was the victim of an acid attack arranged by her ex-boyfriend. She shared these words in an award ceremony to young people where I was privileged to sit next to her.

"We can survive three weeks without food, three days without water, three minutes without air, but we cannot take another breath without hope." **Katie Piper**

These words came to her when she was in agony in hospital. Hope, that is your most important thought. With hope comes all the actions that you can put into place to recover from whatever is hurting you.

CHAPTER 3

You Are in Exactly the Right Place in Your Life

Could you allow yourself to consider that you are exactly where you should be, right now? The past has lined up and made you who you are, and your future is going to be exactly what it should be for you. You are in control: nothing in your past was wrong, everything was right. You are in a great place in your life and it is only going to get better.

Like many, I have struggled, I have suffered anxiety, I have lost, failed, won and celebrated. I have lost myself, I have found myself. I have over thought everything, and I have over analysed my life. I have been angry, I have been sad. I have spent time recovering from burnout, and I have spent time wishing I never had to work again. I have lost my drive, lost my ambition, lost who I am. I have ignored the pain of loss, and I have ignored emotional and physical pain. I am human. I have been scared to really know myself. I know that acceptance of who I am is the key to my future and this has aided my recovery from a bad place. I moved forward in life the moment I could accept myself and accept my journey from childhood through to the current day. I now celebrate all aspects of the adversity I have been through – I am whole because of it.

What I absolutely love about life is that each day is a new day. Each lesson has great learning and, assuming we are fortunate, life is long enough to break, recover and step forward into a new you. The same you, but with new wisdom and awareness.

I have met some extraordinary people who have been through far more than I have. I have also met many people who have said they could not have coped with the stress and grief that I have worked through. Each of our lives is so personal to us – it is our life, and we have to take ownership of it.

No one is the same as you. The complex and beautiful life you have had up to this point is incredible because of each little triumph, and each setback. Now it is time to acknowledge where you are and the decisions you have made in life and discover who you are. Not who you wish you could be. I don't believe you need to change who you are, but I do believe you need to learn to love being you.

Over time we become aware of the four aspects of ourselves. The emotional, mental, physical and spiritual. We are on a journey of all four, and I hope that for all of us the journey is a long one as we are all creating and living our own adventure film and we don't want that film to have an ending yet.

Discoveries

Many of the discoveries I have made about myself have happened through necessity as I was never good at listening to my own needs. When I started to get hooked on understanding myself, I was in danger of overthinking and overanalysing everything. That has been a discovery in itself. I think this saying I see online a lot is a good one: 'Overthinking is the biggest cause of unhappiness. Real life is rarely as bad as the thoughts in our head.' I don't want to lead you down a path of constant self-analysis.

So, there must be a balance. That wonderful word. If we could find balance in all aspects of life, then that must give us peace. But, let's be realistic. Some days we overthink while some things make us overthink, and there are some days when we are too busy to think at all.

I have found that the more I learn about myself, the more that has provided a sense of peace. Of course, there are some things we cannot change about ourselves. For instance, I don't think anything could ever stop me from being over sensitive, driven by my feelings and desperate to love and help people. That is who I am. To some people these may be my strengths and to others they may be huge weaknesses.

The next learning experience was about coming to terms with the fact that I had never achieved the success I felt I was destined for. At one stage, as mentioned in Chapter 2, I was valued through shares in my business at £22m. This created a sense of achievement that I had never sought, and it became the measurement of success for me. When this was far from achieved and life hit the rocks, my inner voice kept telling me that anything less was failure. This played on my mind for many years.

My awakening was that my perceived lack of achievement was not about my failure because, at that time in my life, the most important thing for me was to be good at being a mother. Life is about the values we hold. Yes, I had been the CEO of Ecademy and driven it through the turmoil, and perhaps I could have worked harder, but I would have sacrificed my values of motherhood.

Understanding your own values, the core of who you are, is important to do before you start to define and construct the life you have, or when you look back and wonder why life didn't turn out the way you expected.

Setting the right expectations

Another awakening was the realisation that we cannot all be world-class. The world many of us have built our careers in has been dominated by stories of millionaires and billionaires, especially in the dotcom era of overnight success. I remember coaching a young man who, at the age of 31, had a digital business employing seven people, and he felt totally dissatisfied with his achievements. He was married, had a home for his wife and two children, and yet he was bordering on depression and showed signs of stress due to his lack of achievement.

On talking to him, I discovered that his measure of success, his benchmark, was the founder of Facebook, Mark Zuckerberg, and Elon Musk, quoted as number 21 on the Forbes 2016 Rich List. Coming to terms with being great, not awesome or world-class, can be hard. The young boy who dreamed of being at Wimbledon, the young man who thought he could be the next Tiger Woods. For me, I thought I could be like Anita Roddick, founder of The Body Shop.

There comes a time in our lives when we have to accept our capabilities. This does not mean giving up on our dreams and ambitions, but it does mean peppering them with the reality of who we are and the fact that very few people are giants in this world. We can be a giant in our own world to those we love, to our close community and to our clients.

Success is personal

The moment that I actually realised I was successful was the moment I measured my success against my own personal values. For the first 25 years of my business life as a business owner, I was also a mum to three young children. The values I held as a mum, and the need for me to be with them and give them love, security and time, far outweighed the values for wealth and financial success. When we know our personal values, we learn what success means to us at a given time in our lives.

We can all see our life in stages − it is not one chapter but many chapters. Childhood, young adult, early career, parenthood, midlife, parent to independent adult children, and later life. The point here is that we have more time than we realise. We can still reach the top of a mountain, but perhaps it needs to be done in stages. It can be the rush that causes the stress, and the stress takes away the joy of the journey.

Success at each stage will be defined by the priorities we hold. I am clear now with three adult children that my brain and my energy is on fire and the next stage of my career will be energised and driven by a sense of contribution and also a sense of future security rather than the need to feed many mouths.

During every chapter of our lives, stuff happens. The world spins and changes, and we experience disruption and adversity that remind us to adapt, adapt, adapt.

Do Millennials think differently?

We now live in a transparent, open world, and the shifts in business over the past 50 years have been tremendous. The culture of success and its meaning has also shifted.

Many of the Baby Boomer Generation, born between 1946 and 1964, have been subjected to messages of economic wealth, home ownership, property growth, designer clothes and accessories, and are addicted to displays of wealth that provided a feeling of success, or one-upmanship. There was a need to show that they were successful, but even more was the need to appear more successful than the next person. This generation has also been subjected to an enormous shift in commerce, global political challenges, the launch of the internet and the disruption of business models, along with the decline of the High Street and manufacturing. The level of adaptation is massive.

I sense that Millennials see things differently. Their influences differ from those of their parents, the Baby Boomers. I hope and believe their role models are chosen with a different set of values than the ones we were exposed to. Wealth creation is still on the lips of this generation but their path to it, their mode of working and their definition of success is perhaps more tinged with purpose, contribution, sustainability and lifestyle.

Changing times, changing beliefs

We are in changing times for sure. The definition of success is changing. We cannot blindly seek success without knowing what success means to us personally. The moment when we close our eyes for the last time and say goodbye to the world, what do we hope to have achieved? What would our friends, relatives and even strangers who have followed us online say about us? Success to some would be monetary, fame, power, travel. To others it might be family, relationships, stability, peace of mind.

Are you at the right place in your life?

The torment we put ourselves through is underpinned by our expectations, but I also believe our minds are played with over and over again by our ambitions and desire for success.

I don't think I have ever found the language to articulate exactly what success, ambition and happiness means to me. Yet, the feeling of being unsuccessful, of not achieving my ambitions, and the subsequent analysis of my happiness abounded. The way our minds work is incredible. They can loop on the same emotion and, until we find a way to articulate the emotion, we can never give ourselves peace. That voice, that deep, unarticulated emotion that just sits inside us has the potential to create havoc.

What is success?

Your definition of success is important to you, and it needs to be relatively attainable. I used to have huge, scary goals until I learned that it can have an impact on dopamine levels, the reward system in our brains. We must allow ourselves to achieve success. Therefore, we must define what success means to each of us.

Your personal definition of success will be linked to your values, to what makes you happy, and to your reward centre which releases dopamine when you achieve.

I love this poem by the American poet Ralph Waldo Emerson (1803–1882):

What is Success?

To laugh often and much;

To win the respect of intelligent people

and the affection of children;

To earn the appreciation of honest critics

and endure the betrayal of false friends;

To appreciate beauty;

To find the best in others;

To leave the world a bit better, whether by

a healthy child, a garden patch

or a redeemed social condition;

To know even one life has breathed

easier because you have lived;

This is to have succeeded.

Ambition is personal

To understand the will to succeed, I think we need to also understand ambition. Your ambitions are personal to you and are not linked to how you define success. I see myself as very successful when I measure my success against the values I hold. However, the achievement of my ambitions seems way off. The impact I want to have, driven by my deep desire to help others and make a difference in the world, are yet to be fully achieved. I still want to build a community for business owners that supports, loves and helps them become all that they seek to be. What is your ambition?

"Ambition is a curse", to quote Luke Johnson in his book *Start it Up*. It is a burning inside that is almost from birth. Striving for the unknown and never knowing whether you have reached it or not. I think of it as a mountain I started to climb at birth and I assume the summit is found in death. I don't think ambitious people are ever satisfied. The dictionary states ambition as: 'a strong desire to do or achieve something'. When you combine that with Maslow's Hierarchy of Needs, he states that humans are 'wanting animals, never satisfied'. We soon learn why the human species innovates, pushes and never accepts the status quo.

Happiness

I spoke about happiness in the Being Broken chapter. I think we all seek to feel happy, to have that joyous, carefree feeling every now and again that tells us all is okay. I wrote earlier about how solving problems and overcoming adversity can make you happy. Now I want to share an awesome, quite life-changing piece of information that Russell Butcher, a wonderful friend I worked with at Digital Youth Academy, told me one day about research into happiness. Over coffee, having witnessed my diminishing spark of happiness and the stress I was under, he shared this with me and it was a turning point for me and the start of my deep interest in emotional health.

This wisdom came from a study and a documentary he watched on global happiness.

The three parts of happiness

Russell told me that happiness is made up of three things. If you assume 100% of happiness is your goal then 50% is your outlook on life, your constitution, the person you are in your core. Ten percent represents the achievement of the things we want, short-term things that once achieved, we want again. We are 'wanting' animals as Maslow states, and we advance as humans in a kingdom of animals as we are never satisfied.

Now comes the killer sentence: Forty percent 'is how much control we have over our lives and the decisions that impact us'.

I have always been anti-control. I find 'controlling' people overwhelming, almost bullying. In my desperation to be un-controlling I had put myself in a position where I lacked any control over my life. I mentioned at the start of the book how this is a trigger for knowing that your business is no longer personal to you. Ultimately, happiness can leave you through lack of control. I have discussed this with a lot of my clients, many of whom tell me that a major source of their deep distress has been this one issue. Getting back to happiness means taking control of your life, your dreams and your business.

Motivation and drive

I am curious about the difference between motivation and drive and have found these thoughts helpful.

Motivation

Motivation is a feeling, a desire to achieve something, although the same words appear in the dictionary as ambition. I believe motivation needs to be towards something positive and specific. 'I am motivated to write a blog to share thoughts on XYZ' or 'I am motivated to speak at this event as the audience is the perfect client base for me to help'. Motivation is strongly linked to the word 'why'. Why would we do anything unless we knew the benefit?

We have to find motivation in every aspect of our lives, from having good relations with our spouse and children, to keeping the house tidy. We need to be motivated to deliver a good speech, or to contribute over and above for our clients. These are mini-goals in the life of our ambition. It is a state of mind, and I have found that mental exhaustion, rejection, lack of self-esteem, knock-backs and failures can severely impact our motivation.

Motivation is a human need to achieve in every part of our lives, from getting out of bed, to cleaning our teeth before we go back to bed. When we lose motivation, we are mentally in trouble and we must find the source of that loss and recover it fast.

Have you felt this? A feeling that you just cannot be bothered. Motivation to achieve your ambitions and purpose in life can be knocked severely through failure and rejection. For me, learning how to ensure I didn't completely give up was a daily task during periods like this. Remember Tracey Carr and how she felt so weak when she was broken that she had to take one step at a time? This sense of 'what's the point in doing any work' can creep over us and it is terrifying. We can feel as if we are losing the core of who we are. All our energy goes to our head, overthinking everything.

When your drive can help you – to overcome a loss of motivation you have to learn to drive again

Like many entrepreneurs, every day of my working life I had woken with the same drive: fast, furious, foot down flat on the accelerator with long journeys ahead of me. I treated every day with the same injection of fuel, even when I was running on empty. No wonder I was exhausted and unable to put the key in the ignition. Something had to change. I was living my life in my head, abusing my physical being and I no longer connected with my heart.

The cure came in the form of my enlightening moment, much like a car crash! Some call it burnout, and the number of people I have met who have experienced this is incredible. Even worse for me is when I meet someone heading that way – my purpose is to slow them down. When we find ourselves driving too fast, we must slow down.

How do you slow down and avoid the crash?

I did crash, and I did break. I didn't notice in time. I don't want this to happen to you. To ensure I never drove too fast again, I learned that not all journeys had to be long and they didn't always need me to put my foot flat down on the accelerator. The journey didn't always have to be uphill either, and sometimes it could be in a slow car with the wind in my hair and with the most amazing views.

I discovered pace

The day I started to respect myself and drive carefully is the day I turned my life around. It all started with pace. The act of putting one foot in front of the other. Walking not running, and choosing short distances rather than huge mountains. I realised that I could wake up, consider my day ahead and choose how much fuel to put in my engine. Some days required the high energy, high output stamina of a long uphill drive. Other days, I didn't even need to get in the car. The interesting thing is that I didn't have to change my work life, I just needed to change the way I approached it.

If you consider the way top athletes train, they train hard and they rest. Each rest takes them closer to their personal best. We should never feel guilty about the rests. In fact, we should applaud ourselves for understanding how to become a top performer.

Little wins

In order to enjoy a different pace of life and trusting that I could still achieve, I learned to list the little things I needed to do each day, to tick them off and regard these as little wins. I have a physical paper diary for this very reason – each day is a page. I write everything in it that I need to do, from ironing to birthday cards, to accounts to dynamic tasks. The list is never shorter than 30 things in a day and these make up the whole me. Penny Power, mum, wife, daughter, sister, friend, business woman, dog owner. It represents the whole me and I celebrate the tasks that I achieve, those that complete the whole me each day. This is the manifestation of what I wrote about in 2002, that 'emotional wealth leads to financial wealth'. If I am not emotionally strong, I can never achieve the financial ambitions I need to achieve to maintain the values that I hold dear.

Every day is a development of you

When you were born, imagine you could see the mountain of the life ahead of you marked out by every step you needed to take, every moment you fell back down the mountain, every sunny day, every cloudy one, every person who was the sherpa who helped you up the mountain. I wonder which path we would choose to take: the steep climb or the calm grass-covered slope?

What we would see is that every step had significance. We would see the lessons we learned, the people we loved, the people who pushed us back down the mountain, the protection we needed against the people we needed to avoid. The joy is that we don't know any of this when we are born. We learn, we pat ourselves on the back and we get back up and continue our climb. Nothing stops us from choosing to change the path we may have started out on, from the steep climb to the slope, from the slope to the steep climb. It is our choice and our personal mountain.

What we must do, each day, is keep learning. We need to take our emotional and mental wellbeing seriously and take responsibility for our own choices and journey. This means we need to find ways to become emotionally, mentally, physically and spiritually stronger.

The purpose of this chapter is to ensure that you listen to yourself, know yourself and live the life you want from this point forward. Many people hold themselves back. Being honest with yourself, your dreams and the vision you hold is an important part of knowing how to move forward from where you are right now.

I see these beautiful words appear online regularly:

"Our deepest fear is not that we are inadequate. Our deepest fear is that we are powerful beyond measure. It is our light, not our darkness that most frightens us. We ask ourselves, 'Who am I to be brilliant, gorgeous, talented, fabulous?' Actually, who are you not to be? You are a child of God. Your playing small does not serve the world. There is nothing enlightened about shrinking so that other people won't feel insecure around you. We are all meant to shine, as children do. We were born to make manifest the glory of God that is within us. It's not just in some of us; it's in everyone. And as we let our own light shine, we unconsciously give other people permission to do the same. As we are liberated from our own fear, our presence automatically liberates others." **Marianne Williamson**

CHAPTER 4

Being Alone,
But Not Lonely

"Being deeply loved gives you strength,
loving deeply gives you courage."

Lau Tzu

When I drove my eldest child, Hannah, to university for the first time, I said to her: "Darling, there will be times when you will sit alone in your room. That doesn't mean you are lonely." Being alone is a state, a physical state that can be wonderful, as is learning to enjoy your own company. Love time with yourself as this is a beautiful thing. Loneliness on the other hand is different. That is an emotional state that can physically hurt and damage our ability to achieve our dreams. The danger of loneliness is that it can impact our self-worth and give us too much time to overthink.

Stay connected

Choosing to be in charge of your own destiny and taking control of your life and future is the most fantastic personal human achievement. Taking responsibility for your emotions and mental wellbeing come along with this decision. Negative emotions can creep in if we are not self-aware and treat ourselves with the utmost care. Ensuring we stay connected and maintain relationships, build new ones and retain our sense of self-worth and belonging to society and others is your responsibility. For some people, working alone works, while for others, it can lead to a deep sense of loneliness.

Your five basic needs – what can be more personal than these?

I assume this business you have is a business that needs to make money and is not a hobby. If you are fortunate enough to have all your needs met without needing to make much money from your business, then enjoy it. However, if your business needs to provide you and your family with the basics of a home and food, then it must be taken seriously.

Going back to Maslow and his Hierarchy of Needs. To get a great level of knowledge about this read his book *Hierarchy of Needs: A Theory of Human Motivation*. Abraham Maslow is a respected and well-known psychologist, born in 1908. I think his beliefs around our five basic human needs are absolutely brilliant and I will refer to them several times throughout this book.

Maslow defined the five human needs, and to achieve each one, you needed to have achieved the one before. They are in order: our physical needs of food, water, warmth and rest; our need for shelter and safety; our need for love and belonging; our need for self-worth and self-esteem, which feeds our confidence; and finally, a term he calls 'self actualisation', which is our morality, creativity and ability to problem solve. This all stems from the basic need we all have for growth.

Your business must feed you, provide warmth and you must rest

Your business has the capacity to fulfil all five needs for you. The first one you have to achieve is that it feeds and looks after you and your loved ones. You are the first cost on your cash flow or profit and loss spreadsheet. You might delay when the business can pay you, maybe you have a buffer of savings or a loan or investment. But it must go in. If there is no money for you, then it is not a business, it is a charity or a hobby. You cannot achieve the next step in human needs unless you have the means to feed yourself and have your physical needs met. Your business owes you this from the day you start to work. Take this as a mental note. Your business is in debt to you.

Money is energy

Emotionally and mentally, this is critical. Take this from someone who did not honour this. Money is an energy. It tells you that you have value, that what you did was valuable. It is also the ultimate way of knowing if there is anyone out there who places a value on what you are offering, so it's the most basic barometer of supply and demand. If you can't get someone to pay you then there is something wrong and you need to fix it. Either there is no demand for your products or service, your price is wrong, your marketing is poor or no one knows you exist and trusts you yet.

Feeling in control provides your need for safety

The next aspect of you that your business can serve is a feeling of safety and security. I am going to add the element of 'control' to this second Maslow theory. Your business should give you a sense of control. Your decisions, your choices and your destiny.

There will come a point with your business, and you will know it, when you feel safe and secure – at least one month of income in your cash flow means next month's needs are covered. Creating a financial buffer is an emotional leap in life. When you achieve this then celebrate your incredibleness.

For me, safety and security is also about the emotions you have around people. In an abundant position, we have more confidence about ourselves and we use our gut more. Our gut feelings are powerful and usually tell us if the people we meet are aligned to the values that are important to us. Having the confidence to work with people that are not like us would be an ideal. I am all for diversity of thought, character and ambitions.

When a business relationship challenges your personal security

A client of mine expressed a time when he felt insecure in business, and I want his story to act as an example for you to avoid. My client, I will call him John, found himself in business with people who made him feel insecure. He said he could enter a room they were in and feel intimidated immediately. He tried to describe what they would be doing and couldn't without getting visibly upset. However, on further discussion, it was clear that their mere presence made him feel small and took away his confidence.

It transpired he started the relationship with them in scarcity. He made a business decision based on desperation and began the relationship with them by being overly grateful and unworthy. This created a space between them similar to that between adult and child. Sadly, they were highly assertive and occasionally aggressive, which was a recipe for hell for all involved. This was a huge factor in his business survival because he felt insecure and unsafe in their company.

My client was outwardly bouncy, positive and joyful with me. The change in his persona was so dramatic, it was clear that these people were breaking him, and the relationship was too hard to resolve. Through my observations of his declining happiness, I suggested that he positively surrendered, meaning, he didn't feel he had just 'given up', instead he has made a choice to regain control in his life and accepted that this was no longer right for him. There was no way he could ever change the relationship with these people as they had so much control over him. The moment he made the decision was the moment he felt safe again. This safety came from a place of control – he was back in control of his life.

Even some clients have to be sacked!

The interesting aspect of Maslow's five basic needs is that he believes we cannot move up the pyramid of needs unless we achieve them in order. Once you are financially able to cope with life, you then work out who you can and cannot work with. Being aware of this may give you an objective view. One startup I recently mentored sacked a client. The business owner soon realised that this client was going to be a drain and would inhibit her confidence and growth. She was in scarcity, but she made this decision with an abundant attitude.

Love and belonging

Being a sole trader, starting a business, being a business owner – all of these can be the happiest of times, the best decisions we make. As are making choices that are our choices, working with people we want to work with, fulfilling our dreams and living a life of purpose. I began this journey in 1995. I don't regret it for a single moment. What I wish I had known then, and I know now, is that it can also be lonely. But it doesn't have to be that way as loneliness is a state of mind, while being alone is a choice.

Alone, but not lonely

Loneliness is a sad human emotion. We should never confuse it with periods of being on our own. Loneliness is a chronic feeling of being unconnected, feeling of little value to others and it can result in losing our sense of self-worth in the world. Loneliness impacts drive and motivation. If no one cares, then why bother? I have written these words from my heart as I know this feeling. I have experienced business loneliness and I can slip into it quite rapidly if I am not careful. I need people.

Loneliness in business is very common

I know childhood loneliness, I know the feeling of being isolated in an employed job and I deeply know loneliness in business. I am not alone in this fact. I have conducted a poll and 83% of the respondents said they were lonely or had experienced loneliness in business. I have also interviewed a number of sole traders in an attempt to better understand this. If loneliness can impact our drive and motivation, what impact does this have on our ability to achieve our personal ambitions?

The experience of loneliness in business happens when we lose a sense of belonging. When you work with others in a team, you are a community. You see each other regularly, you speak, share goals, share a vision and seek success together. The important part of this is that you will have value to that group. The part you play, the contribution you make, no matter how small, matters. You matter. When you work alone you are in danger of losing this aspect of human need as you become disconnected.

Don't overcompensate for your lonely feeling

Even more dangerous than being disconnected, you might act out a persona to the world that you are strong, successful and everything is brilliant. In doing this, you put walls around yourself, impenetrable walls that make it hard for anyone to get close or for anyone to make you feel that yes, you do matter. Your internal voice says: 'I don't need anything. There is nothing you can do to matter in my life'. The other person thinks, why bother?

Why do some of us feel lonelier than others?

During my study of loneliness, I met with 10 people who were willing to share their loneliness with me. There were some startling similarities in the level of independence, the fear of asking for help and their isolated childhoods. They also expressed issues around trusting people, having been hurt in the past by those they had trusted deeply. These people were also amazingly giving of their time and attention and were great networkers.

The common theme was their fear of letting anyone in, the fear of sharing a need or a vulnerability. They had each created a wall around themselves that was hard to penetrate. All of them were from the corporate world and had left in order to achieve more balance and friendships. Yes, they were making lots of connections, and they were great at their work, but none had found the deep connections they wanted. They knew a lot of people, but only as acquaintances.

Small is the new big

The corporate world of branding, processes, appearance of perfection and closed, fairly heartless communication has created a commercial world that I feel is imploding. Individuals within large companies feel disconnected from the purpose of the business and from one another. Leadership is confused. The 1980s style of ball-breaking leadership, 'tell and do', lives on within too many companies. Even our TV entrepreneur celebrities have an angry, hard attitude to people and money. This creates a chasm between the enlightened entrepreneur of today and the old-style wealth creators.

It is okay to be heart centred

When people escape the corporate world to become their own boss, you would think they would want to be more heart centred and get away from the corporate culture. Unfortunately, this is not the case, as many, especially when marketing, copy the attitudes that are so indelibly soaked into their being. They create a website that is branded with their company logo, they imply their business is large, they hold on to a closed, controlling and tough belief system, and nowhere do they show the world a softer version of who they really are. They won't go out of their door and say they have started a business until they have all the appropriate stationery. In meetings they talk about 'we' can do this 'we' can do that, passively implying that their business is more than just one person.

Is it any wonder that it is these people who are in danger of becoming lonely?

The power in 'The Power of One'

'The Power of One' is in the passion, purpose and commitment you have. The desire to make a difference, the journey you have been through, the adversity of your journey that gave you empathy, depth, compassion – this is what makes people want to know you and do business with you. I believe trust is the most critical asset to build in a business. We all seek to be trusted and to trust others. Yet, many of us fear being real, honest and raw. Why? Because open communication allows others to see and learn the real you – to connect with the real you.

Times are changing and small is beautiful. If you doubt this, ask any employed person, perhaps even the client who hired you, and they will probably say they would love to be brave enough to go it alone. So never feel small. Remember you are the bravest people in the economy and, increasingly, the economy is saluting you.

Being yourself

You are ready to be a member of this brave community of solopreneurs and business owners when you are ready to be yourself. Those who have been awakened to this reality will spot a fraud a mile off. They will see the actor in you, the person who broadcasts their business, connects for a transaction then moves on with speed to find another person they can thrust their business card on to. We have all been there, fearing the reality of being alone in business and worrying that this makes us small. We are terrified of anyone knowing that we are not winning, that we are struggling, just like everyone else does at some point.

You wanted freedom, so be free

Freedom means freedom of thought, spirit and choice. This must be one of the reasons you chose to start your own business. So be free with who you are, once you have decided to be you. Only then are you ready for the most wonderful part of being a business owner. You can become a member of the business community which comprises 5.5 million people in the UK alone. There are 3 billion people working worldwide and, on average across the list of countries, over 50% are self-employed. That makes one huge community to make friends with.

You have so much to offer

To feel more connected to this amazing world let's consider what assets you have to bring to the business world. Your material assets are of no importance to me or anyone else. Your real assets are your skills, your mental agility, your stamina, your drive, your purpose and your honour and integrity. So, your assets come from your mind, body, heart and soul.

Your ability to problem solve with your mind, be physically well enough to work, kind enough to care and deep enough in spirit to connect. This is what the world seeks: good people, with kind hearts and strong minds, who are physically fit and who can connect with honesty and integrity.

Put those thoughts into your brand and connect with them – be those beautiful things to and for others. You cannot connect deeply, allow others to know and trust you enough to give you work and share their hard-earned money if you are lying to yourself about who you are. Once you have overcome this fear, it is time to connect on a deeper level.

Connecting deeply with your heart

I have met so many people who say they suffer from impostor syndrome, doubting their achievements and feeling they are not good enough. They use the 'fake it till you make it' phrase, a phrase I despise as it asks you to pretend. What a strange thought. And what a pile of stress that places on your shoulders.

Belief in yourself, through the validation of who you are is far more powerful. By deeply considering the person you are, your values, experiences, skills, heart, mind, soul and commitment – these are the things that will give you inner belief. You need to get to a place in your heart where you trust yourself and your intention to others so that you can allow that feeling and desire to make a difference to you and the way you serve others.

I am not saying it is easy, but I am suggesting that it is the best way to find your drive, confidence and belief in yourself.

Impostor syndrome

From 1992 to 1998, I was a stay at home mum. It is amazing how fast our confidence in business can diminish. During that time the internet took hold of business and its processes. I came up with the idea of Ecademy over lunch with Thomas and the children. Then fast forward four years into building Ecademy, where I found myself relatively well known, appearing in the media a fair amount and being saluted for a trailblazing idea of building an online community specifically for business people.

My challenged self-esteem and impostor syndrome were never more evident as the differences between my external self-esteem and my internal became apparent. Externally, I seemed to be on top of the world. Inside my head, I was a starving mum of three, exhausted by fear and physical lack of sleep, conflicted by what I was being displayed as, compared to who I truly was. I found myself surrounded by business people in our community who were far cleverer and more experienced than me. My mask was a smile, my daily drive was based in scarcity and fear. My saving grace was that I had a huge sense of contribution and purpose, and I believed strongly in the message I was taking to the world through the community I was building.

'There are no statues to the critics'

I had my inner voice reminding me of who I was and what I believed in, but I feared sharing it. I feared ridicule and I feared the critics. I needed to find that belief in myself and what I believed about the business world. I needed to stand up and share it. In 2002, my chance came. I was invited to speak at a BT Women's network by an amazingly enlightened lady called Jane Swift. Terrified, but feeling safe in the knowledge that she knew me, I spoke for half an hour about my belief that business people had to become softer, gentler and more caring towards one another. I spoke about how, in a connected world, who we are matters more than what we are, and that through our likeability and an open mindset, we could build great trust.

I said I was terrified, and I was, until Thomas said: "Penny, go and do your thing and be yourself. There are no statues to the critics. If you want to make a difference, you have to be brave and live your beliefs and share them."

In Chapter 10, I write about the importance of valuing yourself, so others can value you. Being able to find your voice and share it is a large part of Maslow's fourth basic need – your need for self-worth, which stems from our need for validation. The link between these two cannot be underestimated. It is hard to belong to communities of people if you don't value yourself. Rest assured this is covered later on in the book.

Finding the core of you

The moment I began to talk about emotional wealth in a strong, scary, energetically different place, there was a powerful shift in my confidence and desire to keep banging the drumbeat of the importance of being you. A few years later, another wonderful lady, Christine Clacey, who was a business coach at the time, asked if she could help me define my true purpose in life by taking me through a process called 'Core Process'. We spent three hours together discussing some great moments in my life and some tough ones, discussing how I felt about them. Through this we came up with two words that summed up my life purpose. Mine were 'connecting hearts'.

Connecting hearts to really belong

To me, the power of 'connecting hearts' lies at the very core of who I am because it is what I believe at the deepest level: we are all happier when we can achieve this level of communication. It inspires trust, and it opens us up to a world where energy flows into our bodies that is far superior to just our minds. Our minds can control us both negatively and positively and can provide us with the gifts of skills and the motivation we need, but our hearts are our greatest friend – our hearts are the core of us. If we can use our hearts well in business, it can calm us and give us meaning. It can connect us to the people who will be the most powerful influences in our lives.

Your business, your purpose, your voice – business is personal

Don't fear what is inside you, don't hide who you are. You are the greatest gift to the world when you set yourself free from the critics. When you speak with your heart, people will listen with theirs.

Whenever I am confused, lacking in inspiration, feeling threatened or doubting myself, I shift my mental energy to my heart energy.

I literally imagine moving it. I take a breath, I empower my heart with oxygen and I can see the world in its best light, where I am the best that I can be. Purpose then fills my veins and my values return. I know that when I use heart energy I am protected, and I am safe. I am truly myself when I am thinking and being through my heart.

I was once told that there are two important days in your life, the day you are born, and the day you discover why you were born – and you will know that when you can find it within you. Take time now to think about it, allow it to emerge over the next few days. It is the voice inside you that you have been too scared to release.

Let's allow this connected world to be real, you can lead from the front

When I reflect on my life journey, I can see that this has always been important to me. From my school days, through my early work life and into entrepreneurship, I have written about emotional wealth leading to financial wealth and have created business communities to help people feel less lonely. I have watched the power of people being themselves, of finding that being themselves is the most powerful person they can be.

We are less connected to more people – can we change the legacy of social media?

The great sadness for me is that the new connected world is not fulfilling the real promise of being connected. The world is connected up like machines. Shallow connections on social media serve more to make us feel small and less beautiful, less successful, less happy… less, less, less. The result is that, despite our global connectedness, we have become less connected to more people. True connection makes us feel more: more valued, more unique, more supported, more loved.

This is what we all need to strive towards. Some are already there, while others pretend to be, with great skills in technical manipulation. Only you know if you are connecting deeply. I know I preach it and believe it, but even I struggle. While I have a deep sense of independence, I find it hard to ask for help because I fear the exploitation of my vulnerabilities. Yet, I know that when I deeply connect, I no longer feel lonely even when I am alone.

We all need validation

I have evangelised, taught, used and been addicted to social media for its ability to reach out, to build a brand and enable people to feel validated. A 'share', a 'like', a comment, oh boy does that help when sitting alone and wondering if you matter to anyone.

I was listening to Oprah Winfrey's Commencement Address from Harvard in 2013 where she stated that, of her over 35,000 interviews with people from all over the world, no matter what success they had had, they all ask the same question at the end of the interview: "Was that okay?" She said she had heard the same thing from presidents, to Beyoncé, from the victims of crime to the perpetrators of crime. The fact is, we all seek validation. We all seek to feel we belong, that we matter, that we are doing okay.

Build social capital

Social media gives us all a chance to say to other business owners and friends: "You were great", "I admire you", "I am inspired by you." This is social media working well. It is well documented as having an impact on our reward centres from a short-term dopamine boost. I watch the younger generation and how addicted the under 25s are to their Instagram likes, measuring their worth by this currency.

There are some people I know who have my back, who care for me and encourage me. They are my social capital asset. However, let's get real – in reality, when I am not online, the majority of my online community don't miss me or need me. Do I really belong to anything when I am publicly online? Or is it only through deep and real connections that we grow our social capital, the asset that we need to hold around us for those times when we need real help?

The real promise of the online connected world

So why did I believe in this online world 20 years ago? I believed in it because I sensed that humans had a deep need to connect. I also sensed that the world of self-employment would grow and the borders around the world would come down, enabling us to globally connect. All this is true. What I didn't count on, and what has come about in the online world, is that we have chosen to use the online world in business for transactions and selling. This is where we are falling down. The original promise of Sir Tim Berners-Lee, the inventor of the world wide web, was for a deeper impact than we are individually achieving. The processes and automation of his promise have been introduced, but human connection is being taken out of the interaction with the use of automated tweets, scheduled broadcasts and funnels that send out automated emails once the engine has achieved your first level of trust.

Social engines are breaking the human code of caring

In Sir Tim Berners-Lee's interview in March 2017, he said: "I imagined the web as an open platform that would allow everyone, everywhere to share information, access opportunities and collaborate across geographical and cultural boundaries. In many ways the web has lived up to this vision, though it has been a recurring battle to keep it open. But over the past 12 months I've become increasingly worried about three new trends, which I believe we must tackle in order for the web to fulfil its true potential as a tool that serves all of humanity."

Berners-Lee's concerns lie with the use of personal data, the spread of misinformation and political advertising. What I think he missed is the moral code for humanity, of caring for one another and showing real interest. Social engines are breaking that human code, and this is where we each have to make our difference.

It is hard to put your heart into automated systems

The use of social media to achieve business goals for business is all fine. I love that I have signed up for newsletters, podcasts and YouTube channels of some amazing people I would never get to meet or have the opportunity to learn from otherwise. When joining this automated world and creating your business within it, the key is knowing when to use your head and when to use your heart. Your heart cannot connect through an automated machine in the same way that you need to connect with your clients and influencers for their deep personal needs of self-esteem, belonging and love.

Isolation is the new norm

The internet is known to have isolated us in so many ways. The decline of the High Street and the community around it, the ability to order online without talking to your local small business shop owner and the ease of connecting via a screen. There is an addictive aspect of social media that stops us from joining offline communities, illustrated by how many couples and families I see on their devices in restaurants.

We all need to monitor our own habits and decide whether they are serving our emotional and mental needs. Without emotional and mental wellbeing, we will suffer and our business will suffer.

The good in social connecting

To balance this, and so you know I am not anti-internet and digital technology, I do love what technology can enable. I love that I can keep up-to-date with my friends who I don't see often by watching their lives online and commenting. I love that I can send my dad, aged 91, photos. He uses WhatsApp, Twitter and Facebook. I love that I can see my beautiful daughter's face on FaceTime when she calls from Bali (her new home). I love our family's WhatsApp group where we all know our day-to-day plans and thoughts.

I love that I can blog my thoughts and share my advice and know that it is reaching some people just at the right moment for them. I love that, through the following I have across the main social platforms, I can build my brand and receive feedback, good and bad. I love that these moments make me feel validated, make me know that in that moment I mattered and was given the attention of others during their incredibly busy lives.

The use of social media and social networking is personal

Recently, I was hired to run a workshop for 64 people to share my thoughts on how to build a profile online. The room was a mix of personalities, business models, attitudes, skills and desires to be inside the online social sites. Some liked Facebook, others liked LinkedIn, Pinterest and Instagram. About half the people in the room clearly did not want to use these sites at all. They seemed desperate to find a way to automate and delegate and not engage with their potential customers.

I worked hard for six hours to persuade the audience of the benefits of real engagement. I could sense there were a number of people who did not want to receive my message, and the conflict in the energy between us was very apparent. I closed the day by saying this: "Social media and connecting is personal. Like all things in business, it is your choice. Find the places your clients hang out, use the platforms the way you wish to, build your reputation and social capital in the way that suits you." We cannot force ourselves to do things we dislike. As humans, we are very good at convincing ourselves that our opinion is the right one, fearing the way we may need to adapt.

If you delegate your social connecting to someone else

I am aware that there is a huge industry in Ghost Profiling, the act of delegating your social media to a third party. Online profile building is very personal. Delegating this aspect of who you are to someone else has to be done with great precision and huge dedication to ensuring your supplier really 'gets' you and your values.

Delegating and setting up systems to be present is better than nothing at all. The only thing we can do is to understand the consequences of not connecting personally, not understanding the connected world, and just hoping that we don't become a disconnected generation. One thing is for sure, the generation coming through are the most connected there has ever been and they are desperate to eat our food! Large numbers of them are creating stories on Instagram, putting up photos in real time and engaging with their followers. They are proud of their businesses and want to talk and share by being themselves.

The power of online communities for belonging

True belonging happens when you feel safe to be yourself and you know that others share your values and want you to be strong and happy. There are some amazing groups that well-intentioned people have created. The culture in these groups works, as their intention is one of support, kindness and caring. The leaders of these are amazing 'servant leaders', creating the groups for all to gain something, and creating the groups in order to serve. I believe we can all lead communities. It doesn't matter how big they are – we can create communities that serve others through our heartfelt intention to serve.

Your personal social audit

The internet is a good place. My message here is to ask you to consider how you are connecting within it, and how this world is serving you. Whether you are addicted to social networks and perhaps should do an audit on this, monitor yourself and your use of it, and ensure it is healthy and is working for you, rather than controlling you. It should not make you feel small, nor should it be hurting you. Remain in control of your experience of the internet, the people you connect with, the news, media and messages you absorb. The danger of the internet is when it controls you.

Compare and despair

"Comparison is the thief of joy."

Theodore Roosevelt

The best way to serve your needs of belonging, and not isolate yourself in order to achieve the version of happiness and success that you desire, is to understand yourself deeply. I have mentioned a number of times that the root of unhappiness can be when we compare ourselves to others. It is so easy to do that online in a split second. We can also do it offline, but there is something more real about the offline world, where we can see the whole person. Online, we see only the one dimension they choose to show.

When we feel great about ourselves, the world is great, we love other people's successes, joy and happiness and we celebrate with them. Life is good.

When we have our low moments, it is easy to jump online and feel as if we are standing still, with the world rushing past, beautiful people, couples in love, holidays, awards, parties – you name it, we see it all. We see the photos and the words they share, and their lives look perfect. We have a 360-degree view of our own lives and only one view of them online. What is more, it is the one degree they are willing to share.

I don't want to look too perfect

I often fear that my brand looks too perfect. Pictures of my husband, three children, travels, speaking gigs, family outings – perfection. You would have to know me to know the reality. The broken parts of me, the grief, the financial stress, the illnesses, the fears and the vulnerabilities. In effect, the real me. When I speak at events, I often start by asking: "Who in the room hates me, hates the perfect life they see?" We all have a tendency to create a belief about people when we look from afar. The reality is we all suffer the same fears, pains and vulnerabilities. We all have adversity to overcome, pain from our past, pain at the exact moment you are seeing their online photo and wishing that were you.

The online world has created a documented mental issue, called compare and despair. It wouldn't have been created as an official phrase unless it was a real mental issue. Be aware and don't be taken in any more, don't compare as it's impossible to compare the whole you with one dimension of someone else.

How can you stop making others feel this way?

I can imagine having read the last section you are wondering how to post anything in case you make someone else feel bad. Knowing this and being the kind person that you are, I'm sure you cannot stand thinking that your online persona would ever make someone feel badly about themselves. To think that in a two-minute snapshot moment any of us could release pain into someone else's life seems crazy. I consider this every time I post.

The conflict in this is that we do not want to come across as a victim. There is nothing more annoying than unsolicited advice from people – plus, most of us would not want to come across as weak and needy. So, how can you stay part of the online world, be connected to it and use it to stay relevant and approachable? This is a really hard one. I have found a way to achieve this, I hope.

I have my own community on Facebook. This is where I am really me – I share my daily emotions, ask questions and reach out for help, and in doing this, it creates a culture where others can do the same. I try to add words into my Instagram and Facebook posts that enable others to share their lives. I may mention that a special day is unique and not my whole life. I do all I can to be real and raw. I guess the thing to ask yourself is: "When I post this, who does it serve?" Be honest with yourself. If it is nothing more than bragging rights, then temper it occasionally, as we all know that the kid in the playground is never really liked, no one ever really gets close to people like that. In other words, is it really doing you good, or could your post actually inspire, give hope, love and knowledge? Now, that is a whole different approach.

The true feeling of belonging

Belonging, the third stage of Maslow, is the stage that comes after satisfying our physical needs and our desire for safety and it's the step before self-esteem. Belonging is a human need. Without a sense of belonging we are lonely. Throughout the book I am addressing the issue of business loneliness – it is an economic issue for you and for society. It impacts our motivation and our drive and can stop our ambitions being achieved.

We know when we have a sense of belonging to something. We sense the fact that we fit in, that we matter, that we can contribute, and this creates a sense of feeling valued. When we feel valued, we build our self-esteem, enabling us to be resilient and stronger, while protecting ourselves against harm and pain. It is important to stress that not everyone needs people around them. But we all want to feel valued.

Belonging is personal – we all need this in different ways

To explain this further, I want to refer to personality types. Many of us have done tests to determine our personality: extrovert, introvert, people- or task-oriented, assertive, or unassertive. Knowing yourself is important. These tests are available free online.

As humans, we all need to achieve a sense of self-worth and to be valued by others. We have achieved this since time began by belonging to social networks, a term around long before the internet! If we don't have this belonging, it can cause all sorts of psychological impacts, a key one being the sense of value in oneself.

The varying personality types gain their sense of value in a social place in different ways. The most common tests such as www.ima-power.com examine your personality from two perspectives: are you task- or people-focused, and are you assertive or non-assertive in your communication.

The four ways people get a sense of belonging

It has been fascinating running communities to witness how each of us will seek different ways to feel validated and gain a sense of belonging. I think it is useful to consider in what way you get a sense of belonging and validation, and to discover the best way for you to achieve self-worth.

Belonging and feeling helpful

If your drive to belong comes from feeling helpful and needed, from listening and solving people's problems, then your feeling of loneliness and disconnection will come when you don't feel valued by others. You need to get feedback that you matter to others and are making a difference. I have witnessed how people like this need people, and will achieve a better sense of belonging in smaller groups. They probably need to meet face to face, or in smaller, private online social groups. This mode of networking is far more intimate as you get to know one another more deeply and with regularity than in many larger groups.

Belonging and achieving success

If you are not as people-oriented and seek to get tasks done, you will enjoy belonging to networks that make you feel you are achieving. Your validation probably comes from knowing and measuring yourself against your peers. Your validation comes from feeling successful relative to those around you. You will naturally seek groups that validate that feeling, and where measurements and success dominate the atmosphere and conversation.

You need a network in order to compete, as this helps your drive and ambition to succeed. LinkedIn groups work well for this personality type where being social is not as important as the business conversations you seek. I have met many people inside 'mastermind' groups like this. I always feel that anyone who resonates with this personality type needs to find social groups, not just business groups. Many of my clients who are this profile also belong to running or cycling groups to relax and find social interaction.

Belonging and the need for autonomy

Autonomy is the feeling of control and freedom, and this is important to people who prefer their own company. If this sounds like you then I suggest you might gain your personal validation by being valued for your knowledge – the accuracy and depth of it. You would like it if people said: 'you were so thorough', and 'you did a great job with that piece of work'.

This personality is introverted, highly detailed and is the least impacted by loneliness. Feelings don't come into the analysis of life, rather the facts and a logical reason for action is what is important. Working alone is enjoyable. If this is you, or someone you know, then the challenge is not to be too isolated at home. Those who work alone may never get the feedback that their work is valued, and critically, they will miss out on business development opportunities. It is important to note that this personality loves to help others and solve problems, so a network is important for their sense of worth and the value they see from others in the knowledge they hold.

The right type of place for this profile is in smaller groups, where the relevance to their knowledge allows them to shine. This group will especially want to network with other like-minded people.

Belonging to create and have fun

If you just love people, get bored easily, enjoy chatting and meeting as many people as you can, then there is a high likelihood that you need people for your drive and creativity. You are an extrovert. Your sense of belonging comes from having lots of people to connect with, and with regularity. This personality type, the high extrovert, needs people more than anything else. Working alone is a real challenge. It is important that the communities they belong to are fun and quite random. They get their sense of value from their interaction with many people by making them laugh and enjoying random conversations. This personality type is most prone to loneliness, but thankfully, they have the best personality to combat it.

I suggest you spend time finding out what your personality traits are and then consider whether you are working with the right strategy to achieve your sense of belonging and validation.

We can't fight the new norm – connecting is for life now

Whatever your personality type, we cannot fight against the social world around us. The world has become more social, which means it is more open, more random and more supportive. My absolute favourite aspect of the online world is the ability for us to be closer to people. For me, the smaller communities online are where I get the most joy because they are where I feel the safest and where I create the longest lasting bonds.

The social capital I have created in my life outweighs the financial capital I have created, and I value it enormously – these are the people who come back into my life through a random moment when we collide again online, where we meet over a conversation, or I put out a request. Just this morning I had a Zoom conversation with someone I have known for 15 years online. We notice each other a lot, but it has been a long time since we had a reason to chat and help one another.

I believe that my social capital is a lifelong asset, built over years and years. I have seen pictures of my social media contacts get married, I've seen their newborn babies, their losses and, yes, I will grow old with them. I never see the short-term in my connections. I never know when I might need them, or they might need me, and I don't judge the reasons, whether emotional or for business.

How we wish to receive and give recognition and validation is personal

Throughout this book, I am aware of the variety of personalities and the characteristics we all have. I want to respect all people and their differing communication styles, values and desires. This is the root of what I want to share. The individuality of us all.

I came across a great questionnaire online formed from the book *The 5 Love Languages* written in 1995 by Gary Chapman. On his site http://www.5lovelanguages.com/ you can take a test to find out the five ways, in order, that you want to receive love. The interesting point about this for me is that how we want to receive it is often how we express it.

The five ways are:

1. Words of Affirmation
2. Acts of Service
3. Receiving Gifts
4. Quality Time
5. Physical Touch

If we take this into the business world we can interpret this as: how do I most feel validated and valued?

We all have sensitivities and triggers that make us feel that we have been appreciated. Giving that validation to others is a contribution to them that cannot be underestimated.

Giving testimonials

Testimonials are words of affirmation, helping someone out is an act of service, sending flowers to a supplier or client as a thank you is about receiving gifts, taking time to listen to someone in need, someone who needs to know they matter and that they have a voice, is spending quality time. Finally, not everyone in business is tactile, but I see an increase in the number of hugs when people greet one another – physical touch. For me, that last one is always appreciated.

I will finish this chapter with a beautiful story that I heard over 15 years ago. I use it often, and every time I tell it, I am energised by it. For me, this story sums up the reason we must connect deeply, whatever our personalities. I mentioned in the Being Broken chapter that: 'the Queen packed my parachute'. This story is why I said that. I think we can all do this for each other.

Packing parachutes

Captain Charles Plumb, a US Navy pilot with 75 missions under his belt before he was shot down by a surface-to-air missile, ejected from the plane and parachuted into enemy hands. He spent the next six years in a communist Vietnamese prison. But, he survived.

Many years later he was sitting with his wife in a restaurant. He says he was feeling rather smug about his life and his achievements. A man who was sitting several tables away walked over and introduced himself, asking if he was the Captain Plumb who had flown a Kitty Hawk and was shot down.

Astonished at this man's knowledge of him, Captain Plumb asked him how he knew this information and the man replied: "I packed your parachute." The thrill of meeting this man was overwhelming, because he had saved his life.

That night Captain Plumb lay in bed wondering how he had treated that man, a sailor, while he had been a jet fighter. It worried him. I quote: "How many hours did he spend on that long wooden table in the bowels of that ship weaving the shrouds and folding the silks of those chutes? I couldn't have cared less... until one day my parachute became his responsibility and he packed it for me."

At that point, Captain Plumb realised that one's successes are not purely down to ourselves, but to the amazing people who pack our parachutes every day.

That aspect of this story is so powerful in today's highly connected and hugely competitive world. We all seek to survive in our own way. We rush through life and feel compelled to do things that keep us relevant and connected. Yet, the true meaning of connection to me is to pack other people's parachutes whenever I can. A kind word, a thoughtful gesture, noticing a post or giving words of encouragement – none of these take long when we are connected online, but they are worth so much to the person on the receiving end. I think of all the people who want to automate and treat social media as a machine, and how they are missing out on the joys and connections to a life they are creating.

With this thought, remember that every time someone does these things for you, they are packing your parachute, which must give you a sense of belonging and that you do matter.

Completing Maslow's five basic needs

I started this chapter talking about the five basic needs in Maslow's Theory of Human Needs. This chapter has been dedicated to the third need, the need to belong, to be alone, but not lonely. Maslow has two more needs, the fourth level, the need for self-worth and self-esteem, which I touched on in this chapter when discussing the motivation to find your voice. I will be discussing this more in Chapter 10, about valuing yourself so others can value you.

The fifth and final basic need is to find your way to realising your personal potential and lead with the desire to help others, and the need to give back and achieve the full potential of yourself. This is in the final chapter: Your Future Is Personal.

The journey I have taken you on so far has been to motivate your commitment to the notion that business is personal, and to share the ways business can break you in order to help you avoid them, or to feel more normal if these things have happened to you. I hope by now you do feel more confident in being in exactly the right place, and that you have an awareness that it is the whole you that the world wants, not a version of yourself you think the world wants.

The next chapter begins the healing discoveries that I made on my journey: to gain a strong mind so I could once again build a strong business, with a higher level of awareness and a dedication to healing. I know the seven discoveries I made helped get me to the stage where I could grow.

CHAPTER 5

Healing is Personal

Healing discoveries

Life is a journey of discovery of our own personal challenges and achievements. Each action in our lives creates an imprint on our hearts and minds and creates our story. The ideal is to manage our lives carefully, so we can spot the times when we may be heading in the wrong direction and find those moments of awareness when we know our minds are not working positively for us.

Our emotional, mental, spiritual and physical habits are critical to our overall wellbeing. Ideally, we can prevent any progression into real mental health illness. I think I caught myself just in time by realising that a slight shift in my wellbeing was a sign that I needed to take heed.

As your torchbearer, I have to share and indulge in my own being broken moment. I was not clinically depressed, but I am grateful for the warning I received. When I look back, there were definitely 12–18 months when I was not my best self, but I could function, with an occasional bout of my worst self showing its face. This chapter is the part of the jigsaw that began the journey of healing. There were little discoveries learned that saved me from a complete breakdown, making the recovery time faster.

I call them discoveries because they were tiny shifts in my awareness that could make a difference to my wellbeing. I'm sharing them with you in the hope that each of these seven discoveries can become part of your wellbeing too.

All the people I mention here, and in subsequent chapters, have each given me permission to mention them by name. I mentioned in the Being Broken chapter that I found my own Earth Angels, my personal mentors. They all live near me in the South of England. I worked with a psychologist called Dr Anna Collins from the Psychology Clinic in Farnham, and for a short time at the end of my healing, I joined a wonderful group therapy course called Acceptance Commitment Therapy at the Esher Groves clinic, led by Dr Ian Drever. I found the group sessions wonderful, and I loved learning from individual discussions I had with Anna. I have made a decision to see Anna at least four times a year – the habit of checking in with my emotions is now something I respect and see as a positive way to live my life. Just like checking other aspects of my health, I see this as a critical part of my wellbeing.

Wherever you are in the world, you can learn about this subject from people around you, from books and from reading online. Find your own Earth Angels, be your own torchbearer, and if there are parts of my discoveries that you would like to go and discover for yourself, then reach further into those aspects that resonate with you. I have added links to books and websites in the reference area and on my website, and I will update this as I discover more books, TED Talks and people.

Seven moments of self-healing discovery

I have tested and discussed these discoveries with many clients and business friends. They are common and easy to address. These are areas of business life that I wish I had been aware of before I became a business owner. I share them here so you can anticipate any of these situations and can assist you with making your business life easier.

First discovery – you are not infallible

My first stage of self-discovery was that I was not infallible. I could break, and I could be managing things in the wrong way. I could only take so much and eventually my mind, soul and body needed a rest. All entrepreneurs, particularly of a certain age, believe that the route to success stems from hard work and an almost personal destruction in order to wear the badge of honour that says: 'I almost killed myself to build this business'. The personal sacrifice people make can be regretted later. Self-awareness, the experiences I had and the learning that came from them should enable a healthier input and a far greater outcome.

I had three great mechanisms that I used to overcome my pain, and I have now learned the darker side of these. Resilience, my independent streak of never asking for help and the ability to shut pain away.

Resilience – we can break

We know that resilience is a critical mindset for all entrepreneurs as we have to be strong against adversity, whatever large or small knocks we receive. I think, to some extent, we know we have it in us as life throws us knocks from a young age, from the playground to the shock of not passing exams, to the sadness of rejection with boyfriends and girlfriends – all these build our trust that things will get better and the hope that we remain strong enough to see the tough times through. I think my high levels of resilience are also from the independent way I dealt with my sad moments as a child. I guess my mum made me resilient from her lack of emotional attention. I would not advocate that as a way to build resilience in a child though, as the neglect throws up other issues!

Some knocks are harder to recover from though. During my period of reflection and stepping back a bit, I didn't feel resilient. Even an impatient person putting a finger up at me in my car could wind me up. There have been times when I have asked myself again and again, why am I not more resilient? What is wrong with me?

The definition of resilience is the ability to bounce back. So sometimes we have to accept that bouncing back will take time. We cannot expect to bounce back from disappointment or loss as fast as we demand of ourselves.

We just keep going

Many of us keep going when we have our own business. We cannot delegate to a team member, claim sick pay, have holidays, or afford the support we need. We endure, we remain positive, and we maintain our hope. I strongly believe that hope, purpose, and the vision you hold for your business life will be the greatest way to get back up after a fall. I also know that it was the social capital I held in my life through all my business connections and friends that helped me to believe in myself.

Inability to ask for help – being far too independent

Throughout my childhood, my mum taught me to be independent and to deal with my pain myself. My mum was awesome, dutiful and amazing, however, she did not do emotions. Many a time I can remember being in my bedroom and solving my own fears, sadness and pain. I was not aware that others had a mum they could talk things over with. I never felt sad about this, but I did learn not to ask for help. I lived in an isolated village, the youngest of four children and, through my challenging teenage years, I had few friends that I could see out of school, no siblings at home and a mum who was dealing with her own challenges. By the time I was 14, my mum had been a mum for 26 years. Nurturing and the demands of parenting runs its course, I guess. None of this was the fault of anyone, it was just how it was.

I mentioned earlier that business loneliness can be created by the independent streak that so many of us have. We fear being needy, looking like a victim or appearing weak. I covered the solution to this in the chapter Being Alone But Not Lonely, where I had a great feeling when I asked for help – and by magic my Earth Angels, my mentors, appeared.

Ability to shut pain away – telling myself not to think about how I felt

I have an innate ability to tell myself that I am positive, and that life is okay. In other words, I can shut out pain and frustration and take myself back to positivity. I bet you do too. None of us want to feel crap. This skill is a great one, and yet it is a destructive one in the long term as a way to survive most of the daily ups and downs.

Why don't you just stop feeling that way?

How many of us start a business in our 30s when we are also having children? We seek to manage a social life, have parents and commitments to others and joyfully believe that we are completely infallible.

At 34 years of age, I started this journey and began the experience of absorbing stress as an adult – real, dangerous stress. At the time, I was in startup mode, building Ecademy. I had three young children, a puppy, and the beginnings of money worries for the first time. I was at my computer a lot, through the night when the children were asleep, neglecting to sleep the hours I needed and inevitably suffering with a bad neck. I guess you are nodding your head right now. This is normal.

I went to see an osteopath. On my third visit, he announced that the appointment would be a conversation rather than the usual hands-on approach. He asked me what was going on in my life. I shared the tiger-by-the-tail experience of starting Ecademy, my young family, the puppy, and my constant juggle of school and nursery runs, all of which were average and normal challenges. Then he then asked me: "How do you feel?" I said I felt out of control and stressed, and his reply was: "Well then, stop feeling that way."

The empowerment I got from this brief interaction was enormous. Was it really that easy? From that day in January 1999, I decided that whenever I felt sad, stressed, exhausted or overwhelmed, all I had to do was to stop feeling that way.

'You are the strongest, most positive person I know' was an accolade my husband and friends would use, and I wore that badge with such pride.

I hope that, while you read, you realise the terrible error in all of this. First, we should never set ourselves up to be invincible. Second, we must always acknowledge and experience the pain we go through and be able to articulate those experiences. We need to find a way forward with the lessons we are learning and allow ourselves to rest, accept, and look forward with new growth.

Second discovery – rewrite your past with pleasure

I found that the thoughts looping through my brain focused on the pain we had been through. I could take a breathless moment to share a list of things that had happened, but it all sat like a bag of pain on my back. Before I was ready to heal, I found I was doing this all the time.

The important thing was to take responsibility for my life, noting the great lessons I had been able to learn that would make me a wiser business person, seeing some of the outcomes with fewer expectations and celebrating some of the joys that we had created. That included all the pats on my own back as well as an appreciation of those things that I have not handled well. These are all the right things to do to begin the road to recovery, and they are also a critical step in ensuring you don't keep repeating the same mistakes.

One day I told Thomas that I needed to rewrite my past. I needed to include all the positive filters that my past deserves. I did this – I changed my language, which includes taking away some of the blame I was storing. I took responsibility and saw the light in my life that had been there for years and realised how I had placed a dark cloud over it all.

You can do this too. You can put a smile on your face and look back. Write down the moments of learning, which inevitably have caused you pain, and put the joy back into your past.

Third discovery – you can positively surrender

I knew I needed to heal. That was a discovery in itself. I surrendered to the need to be deeply happy again, and it began with many duvet days. I started this process with a lot of guilt over not working at the pace I was used to (who I was guilty to, I have no idea). The biggest shift was that I opened up to deep vulnerability. This was a chosen state of mind that allowed the right people, messages and healing to happen. I had to be proactive. I am aware that someone could lead me to water, but I had to drink.

My healing started in my writing

I was so fortunate to have a community of amazing people that I loved at The Business Café Global group on Facebook. I began to write a post every day about the thoughts I was having. Some were painful, some were vulnerable and some were joyful. I hoped that I was inspiring the other members by being normal. My dream for the community was that we would lift each other up and rise together.

I wrote 60 days of thoughts, one day at a time. I would wake and consider my emotions at that moment as a business owner and share them for discussion. The comments, empathy, learning, validation and the belief in me gave me so much strength. I adore the members of this group. I hope to serve them all for the rest of my life. They are my business family. In sharing my vulnerabilities in this safe place, I was also creating the culture for other business owners to do the same.

I also started loving Instagram posts with spiritual meanings, words that serendipitously spoke to me. I guess this meant I had opened up to the same words that had previously passed me by with no impact. The other comforting part was the recognition that in writing the words, there were others who felt the same way. It helped me articulate in my own mind the feelings I was having.

Fourth discovery – baby steps

I don't believe in overnight change. They say if you want to lose weight for life, do it slowly by changing your habits and relationship with food. It is the same with wellbeing. New habits, new ways of thinking, new behaviours have to be formed. They can't be forced. Healing is personal to you. Your own way, your own pace and what works for you.

It took me eight months to form new habits and I am still making sure I check myself for bad habits creeping back. I talk more about this in the next chapter about emotional and mental healing being personal.

The one huge monster in my life was our financial wellbeing. My relationship with money, my lack of understanding of it, and ultimately my ability to take control of the monster that lay beneath our bed was key. I had to slay it.

Fifth discovery – knowing what your trigger is

Knowing your dominant trigger for stress and worry helps you to make friends with it when it surfaces. For me it was financial stress, which was linked to my deeply embedded need for security.

When I left home at 19, I earned enough money to still have a private health plan and at 20 I bought a house. At 22, I took out a private school fees policy for any children I might have. I was insured to the eyeballs and denied myself many of the young years of madness and freedom, all for the sake of knowing I would be financially secure. When we hit financial insecurity in 2007, this impacted my very being. It all comes down to what values you hold. Your dominant trigger may be very different.

If we look at Maslow and his Hierarchy of Needs again, the ability to feed yourself and your family, have a roof over your head and the need for safety are the two most basic human needs. When they are taken away, the ability to belong, have self-esteem and self-worth and the ability to truly contribute to others is hard. Fighting selfish thoughts, negotiating from a place of abundance, all of these things then become unnatural. They become forced and part of your strategy. My deepest values are to create family (community), to love and to contribute. The fight between my values and survival was in constant conflict.

Make friends with your monster

Seeing the monster that is in your head is the only way to get past it. You cannot ignore it and the first stage of recovery was to learn how to slay my monster. For me, this began with educating myself on the flow of money so I could predict, take control, and look my monster square in the eye. I had to learn how cash flowed. I suspect this is the largest monster inside most entrepreneur's heads.

To many business people this would seem a basic business need. However, there are many thousands of us who do not know how to do this. Managing money is increasingly being taught in schools, thank goodness. I have taught my children to create a personal cash flow, a year of outgoings and incomings, to show them the balance at the start of each month. When I did this with our finances, I projected our debts and our income for three years. As soon as I did this, the monster became real and manageable, and I couldn't deny its presence. At last I could look him in the eye and say: 'One day you will be gone'.

Facing the challenge in our lives that dominates most is brave, it can be painful, but it is critical.

Who is your monster and what does it look like?

Spend time thinking about your monster – your dominant thought and fears. Give it a name and take control of it.

Sixth discovery – fight for happiness

All the tips so far are about practical actions and thoughts. They can give us the calm that can be brought back into our lives and allows us to consider the spaces in our lives that make us happy. In the chapter on Being Broken, I shared the great message my work colleague Russell gave me about the three components that make up happiness. Your constitution, your achievements and the ability for you to be in control of your own life and business. Happiness is not a rite of passage for any of us. But we can choose to have it as one of our desires and seek out the ways we can feel happy.

Your happiness is personal

Whatever it is that gives you that moment of peace, joy and relief gives a sense of happiness. I can find the anchors in my life that I know will bring me this feeling – my children, my husband, my sisters and my close friends. Also, the feeling of delivering a good speech, or helping a client shift forwards in their life.

We should notice those moments – the exhilaration of happiness may last just a moment, but it is the best version of you.

We are not entitled to happiness throughout life. Happiness comes from those moments that are also peppered with challenges: the highs against the lows, the abundant moment of knowing you are in the right place, at the right time and everything fits. Some call it being in the flow. The coincidences show up – those moments when you cannot believe that life seems so easy.

My daughter, Hannah, gave me the most perfect words the day she moved to Bali after deciding to leave the safe corporate world to start the joy of building her own business. She was referring to a close friend who was 'putting up with a job that was not great, living a life that was not great'. She said: "Mum, what frustrates me about this person is that they aren't fighting for their happiness." She looked me in the eye and said: "Mum, you have to fight for happiness."

Happiness starts inside as a feeling and spreads to our faces. I know I am a happy person who sometimes has unhappy moments. When those happen, I acknowledge and respect the reason I have an unhappy moment, and then I fight to get back to the place that gives me that.

Years ago, I read *The Alchemist* by Paulo Coelho. It is a great story. The main character travels the world to find happiness until he returns to the same spot he left and realises that happiness is in us. It is not somewhere else. It is our responsibility to ourselves to find it. We cannot delegate it or expect anyone else to give it to us.

Seventh discovery – letting go of control

In 2009 Thomas discovered the power of letting go of control and the expectations of outcomes. We set ourselves up all the time with the expectations we place on our ambitions and all the work we do towards that expected euphoric moment. We write proposals, go to meetings, network, give huge amounts of ourselves in the hope that our directed energy will create the desired result. The fact is, life is unpredictable and people are unpredictable. We cannot control our outcomes, we can only control our input.

This is far easier to say than to do. But the relief I feel spreading through my body is a physical release. When life hits me in the gut, I say to myself: 'it is what it is' or 'just let go'. There are so many elements to every goal and activity we work towards, and when we try to over control the outcome, that is when stress creeps in and can build our anxiety levels.

I came across this perfect quote online while I was preparing to write this book, and I kept it for exactly this moment. I want to thank Mark Manson for writing a great article entitled 'Why all the best things in life are backwards'. This is a powerful quote from his article.

"Teach your mind to stop chasing its tail... and how do we do this? By letting go. By giving up. By surrendering. Not out of weakness. But out of a respect that the world is beyond our grasp. By recognising that we are fragile and limited and but temporary specks in the infinite reaches of time. You do it by relinquishing control, not because you feel powerless, but because you are powerful. Because you decide to let go of things that are beyond your control. You decide to accept that sometimes, people won't like you, that often you will fail, that usually you have no f**ing clue what you're doing."

I have learned that the seven healing discoveries I listed above were small shifts in my thinking and my emotional wellbeing. I kept them close to me, wrote them as small sentences to repeat until they were a habit and I made them part of me.

The next chapter builds on these seven discoveries and explores our emotional and mental wellbeing. The practical steps above help us towards this wellbeing. Now I want to share with you what I have learned about how some of our emotions work.

CHAPTER 6

Emotional and Mental Health is Personal

Emotions are critical to survival and they help us to experience life. We should never deny the emotion we feel or close it down. Being emotionally closed is not healthy for you or anyone close to you. We have to understand our emotions and know when they are working for us and when they are destructive. In business, managing our emotions is the best way to cope with situations we find ourselves in.

Managing our emotions starts with understanding our relationship with them. When our emotions get out of control for a period of time, this is when we can start to be at risk of anxiety, depression and stress. Three clinical disorders that we all want to avoid.

There is a TED Talk by Ruby Wax who says: "We are not equipped for the 21st century." In this talk she amusingly, but with a serious take on mental health, shares that when we lived in primitive times we would kill or be killed, eat or not eat. Now, in the sophisticated age that we live in, we still feel danger, but we cannot use the adrenalin that gets released when we feel the danger. Instead of fight or flight, the adrenaline lives in our heads like a continuous loop. She states that the hormone adrenalin that once kept us safe now drives us insane.

I would suggest that if any of this chapter resonates with you, spend time considering it and then find someone professional to discuss this with. It might trigger something that needs to be investigated by you. Welcome this into your life and don't deny the opportunity to develop your emotional strength.

Your emotional values are personal

My experience of repair started with the emotional aspect of my wellbeing. I began to doubt my emotional values and many defences began to appear. This was not a sudden discovery. I would say it started four years before I was able to write this book. As you know, I took all of this seriously and found the right people to help me heal so that I could heal myself. I was able to discover these things through various means: the trigger of an Instagram post I read, a TED Talk, a conversation with a friend and the choice I made to see a professional.

I am going to cover four areas of emotions that have impacted my business career:

1. Thought, beliefs and feelings

2. Anger

3. Love

4. Trust

Our thoughts, beliefs and feelings

Our emotions are made up of these three elements. The thoughts that come into our mind, often challenged by our beliefs, and as a result we experience feelings. These can all be positive or negative thoughts, beliefs and feelings. More often than not, we have a voice inside us that makes us worry, regret, fear, become defensive or sensitive and these can impact the way we handle situations.

How your beliefs can work for you or against you is a powerful thing to learn. A psychologist asked me, and others in a group session I joined, to complete this sentence: "I am…"

We each completed the sentence. These are the "I am's…" from our room.

'I am selfish'

'I am clever'

'I am a happy man'

'I don't matter'

The 'I am selfish' belief system meant that this young lady had spent her life giving, rescuing others and overcompensating for the belief that she was selfish. This lovely lady had two autistic brothers who had needed so much attention from her mother and father that whenever she asked for anything, she felt selfish.

The 'I am clever' man had set himself a huge expectation that whenever he failed he found life terribly hard.

The 'I am a happy man' said he was always happy. Yet if anything happened in life that made him feel unhappy, he tended to react very strongly and would be reduced to feelings of despair and low moods.

Then there was me: 'I don't matter' said the voice inside me that had struggled with this feeling. I had lost resilience and found rejection in business very tough. This belief system meant I experienced every business negotiation and sales or investment pitch with emotional investment attached to it.

Completing the sentence 'I am...' is incredibly powerful. The revelations that come from our belief systems can be an interesting discovery, as is the knowledge of how this works for us and can work against us. Remember, knowing that these are just beliefs, born from a period in our lives when they started, means we will know what triggers this belief system into action, which in turn goes on to impact our thoughts and feelings.

Understanding anger

In 2014, I met an amazing lady, Ruth Paris, who has since become such a dear person in my life. She saw me speak at an event and asked if we could meet for coffee. We discovered that she had skills in business coaching, while mine were around social media and personal online brand building. We shared stories of our lives – important for both aspects of our skill-swap.

I shared many highlights of my life, the good and the bad, and told her how important love was to me. How deeply I love, how love is such a beautiful energy, how it heals, forgives and allows people to shine. Much of my story was speckled with the pain of disloyalty from others, aspects of my childhood, the trolls I had experienced in business, the psychopath I was in business with and needed to escape from, and the aggressive investors that I was dealing with at the time we met. She asked me if I ever felt anger, as I hadn't used the word once. I proudly announced that I never felt anger. I told her that I fear anger and cannot deal it.

Anger is not bad

For me, this is one of those milestone lessons in life around emotional health. Anger is not bad. In fact, we need it. It is the trigger in our brain that tells us we need to protect ourselves. It is the emotion we need to ensure that we maintain control of a situation and step away or negotiate an outcome that is good for us. Ruth went on to explain how the limbic system, the emotional cortex of our brain, manages our emotions.

Ruth settled my mind. She explained that to feel anger does not mean we have to be angry with others. Emotionally intelligent people use internal anger to discuss and assert their choices and free will. They use it to protect themselves and create the emotional boundaries that ensure this.

This newfound understanding sat with me for several years, but I never took it further in my learning. I still feared assertive people. I allowed assertive people to control me and found that my best route out of any assertive conversation was to step away. Much like Tracey Carr, who I introduced earlier in the book, I avoided any conflict. I believed my more passive way of communicating was more respectful. What I didn't realise until I started to see a psychologist was that assertive people are great, providing you also have the skills to be assertive. Years of living with assertive people as a child, years of being in business with assertive people had clouded my understanding of communication.

The pendulum between good communication and bad communication is vital to learn. At one end is the passive person, at the far end is the aggressive one. In the middle is the assertive person. True respect is shown in any conversation when two people can both share their needs, desires and opinions while respecting the other person.

In a role-play session with Anna, my psychologist, she showed me the difference. We began a conversation, and I disagreed with her point of view, asserting my thoughts calmly, and then as part of the role-play, Anna responded quite aggressively. I dissolved into tears and started to shake. My reaction was a shock to me. It took me about 15 minutes to calm down. My instinct was to walk out of her room, but of course I knew not too. In any other situation, I would have done that or would have become a wallflower, allowing the other person to win and beat me down. Many, many times this has happened to me.

Assertiveness is about protecting yourself and taking back your control

Anna explained that when someone becomes angry, we have every right to take back control and calmly say: "I am not comfortable with the way you are talking to me. I would like to draw this meeting to a close. I am willing to meet again when you can speak to me calmly." Again, this is about regaining control, it is not about submitting. When I look back at my business relations in my second business, I only wish I had been stronger and wiser. Critically, I bet they wish I had too as it is equally as irritating for an assertive person to have to deal with a passive person. Both need to learn better communication skills.

It is too easy to dominate unassertive people

I share this experience as there will be two types of people reading this book. The assertive and the non-assertive. The confusion between these two in communication in business can be massive and can create misinterpretation and painful dialogues. Knowing when someone is being assertive rather than angry is a short distance for an unassertive person who is easily dominated. We will know which 'type' we are and we should adapt to the other. Allow for the difference. But never cross the line into angry communication in business. Too many of my clients have experienced bullying and intimidation and that is not acceptable at all.

Primary and secondary emotions

Anger is a primary emotion for many types of secondary emotions. The secondary aspect of this emotion is how you feel it. You may say you are angry, but to resolve this you have to feel the secondary emotion. For example, do you feel fear, hurt, humiliated, frustrated or rejected? I have learned that I cannot resolve some of the past experiences in my life until I know the exact feeling they have created in me. For me, believing that I never felt angry was an error. I just didn't know how to articulate the feeling.

Managing anger in others

How we deal with business encounters, disappointments and frustrations is an important emotional skill. It is normal for life to go wrong at times. It is normal for two people to see things from their own point of view.

To ensure we learn from all encounters and achieve harmony, we need to listen without defending and without judgment. We need to understand that the anger someone may be expressing could have its feet firmly in their feelings, fears or loss of control themselves.

If we also embrace how a situation made us feel, we then ask ourselves: can we change and learn from this in order to manage this situation differently when it occurs again?

Learning to notice the early warning signs of anger is a very powerful skill, not just in yourself but in those you interact with. When you notice teeth clenching, jaw tension, or withdrawal for example, you will know that something is creating an angry reaction. It is always better to resolve this early, diffuse and support yourself or the other person.

If anger is an emotion you would like to explore, I suggest you seek out a professional and enjoy the learning and the personal growth you will achieve.

Love

We all want love. Deep down, it is the most amazing human connection. We all want to give love. Somewhere along the way, partly due to life experiences, partly character, we create a view of what love means to us.

When I started talking about love in business back in the 1980s, I'm sure I was seen as a fruitcake. It worked though because I had an amazing career by loving people, and it worked for me. When I wrote about love in blogs in the early years of the 21st century, I could tell many people thought I was too soft and too girly!

Love is a wonderful thing though. To care for someone deeply and want them to be happy, to shine and to have joy, these things give us a sense of self-worth. Often, the love we give out reflects back in the communication and relationships we form.

Love does not have to be unconditional

My lesson in all of this was the addition of the word 'unconditional'. Later in this chapter, I write about 'overdone strengths'. Clearly, love is an overdone strength of mine. I spent my life as an adult, and possibly as a child, believing that everyone deserved love and that I had to love the people I knew, unconditionally. Once again, I didn't consider the needs, wants and desires of myself. I didn't consider the way these people treated me and whether they deserved my compassion and love.

When I talked this through with Anna, my psychologist, she helped me see that my love of my children is healthy – unconditional love is a great bond with a child. However, she questioned me on whether anyone else should have it from me.

How many of us who love deeply hold love as one of our deep values and have a deeply held belief that we can love despite the way someone treats us?

With love comes responsibility. A connected belief to love is to be the person who solves other people's pain, one who takes responsibility for helping people we love and placing a heavy burden on our shoulders. The common belief system of a loving person is that they should be there for anyone whenever they are in need. This is an impossible expectation of self as you will ultimately be torn many times by the needs of too many people. The result is that our own needs are pushed to the bottom of the pile and are rarely tended to.

Love can place dangerous expectation on relationships

The danger of over loving is undoubtedly the expectations it places on a relationship if that love cannot be expressed, shown or is not reciprocated. In the lead-up to my awakening moment, the moment when I knew I needed to learn more about how to take care of myself, I was deeply let down by someone who I had loved unconditionally, a person who had suffered great pain through loss and to whom I had devoted several years of my time and heart. I was resigned to the business world being harsh. However, when my personal life was impacted with the same sense of injustice and imbalance, I realised that I had to adjust my own ways of sensing and protecting myself.

Trust

When trust returns, so does faith, one of the three pillars of living: faith, hope and love. To trust people and your future provides the gateway for your ambitions and your happiness. I think if trust exists, you can open yourself up to the world, take risks and have the energy and the resilience we all seek. I have always been a very trusting person. I rarely do any due diligence on people, believing their values will be the same as mine. Integrity and trust are high on my list of values.

At a networking meeting, I opened up the floor to talk about loneliness in business. I wanted the attendees to share with me the cause and effect of loneliness in a business context. People shared the root of this around high levels of independence, fear of vulnerability, lack of skills in networking, access to people if working remotely, culture and character traits. All excellent input. Then a wise man, waiting for his moment, said: "Trust… when you lose trust in yourself and in others."

His words went through me like a knife. I discovered at that very moment that I had lost the trust I once had and while I thought this would protect me, it had isolated me and stopped me from believing in people and outcomes. It also took away my faith.

Faith, hope and love

The bible declares (Hebrew 11:1): "that faith is the substance of things hoped for and the evidence of things not seen."

Faith, hope and love. These three words mean a huge amount to me. My conversations with my clients tend to enable them to see that there is always hope. They find ways to love themselves and others. The final test of these three words is faith. To be able to hope for the things you cannot see.

Many broken people have lost faith in their future. Faith is an inner confidence that everything will be all right in the end, even if you have no evidence of this fact. Without faith, we take the knocks really hard. Often we have lost faith in our unseen future, and we have to rebuild trust: trust in ourselves, trust in others and trust in our effort.

I shared this issue with my Facebook community recently and was astounded by the connected thoughts of other business owners. One contributor, David Cook, sent me to Chapter 3 in *Think and Grow Rich* by Napoleon Hill entitled Faith.

This quote is very powerful: "Faith is the head chemist of the mind. When Faith is blended with the vibration of thought, the subconscious mind instantly picks up the vibration, translates it into its spiritual equivalent, and transmits it to Infinite Intelligence, as in the case of prayer."

Later in Chapter 8, Spiritual Habit is Personal, I look at the differing practices that can bring us back to faith. Knowing how to calm your soul is a great practice in life. I have had conversations with a church leader about faith; to me, this is a constant challenge, but I have faith in my ability to accept my lifelong challenge.

Faith through purpose

To have faith is a beautiful milestone to achieve and it is work in practice. Many people wrote to me saying they had achieved this in their business when they knew they had a greater purpose, when they could see the mountain ahead that they were climbing and accepted that it was a huge, lifelong mountain to climb. They knew it would be long and tough, but they could visualise the summit. They had their 'why'. When we have faith that we will reach the top, we can overcome the obstacles of life and faith will be restored.

Trust is the greatest asset

The strangest thing is that I have spoken for years about the need to build trust. In my coaching and teaching about building online brands and communities, trust is always at the centre of my work. When people trust you and your brand, it means they know you have integrity, that you are reliable and that you will be honest and open in your dealings with them. Surely this is the world we would all love to exist in.

Reputation takes years to build and a single email to break

A sad fact of life is that it can take years to build your reputation of trust with people. For people to truly know they can rely on you and trust you with their vulnerabilities and know that you will be there for them through thick and thin. I know from witnessing many people who, for one reason or another, acted with a short-term view of life. Perhaps they are in scarcity, perhaps it is just a moment in time when they are angry with the world. The damage that can be done to your reputation in a connected world can be highly destructive. We must all try to manage our emotions and take a breath and sleep on a situation before we react in haste.

When you stop trusting others

We can also lose trust in our own judgment and belief that the majority of people are good. Once trust is broken through the actions of one person who you have trusted, it is hard to come back from this. You lose the trust you thought you had in your ability to gauge people. You lose the trust in yourself to make the right decisions. Ultimately, you decide to isolate yourself for fear of repeating the same mistakes.

Trust and hope

It is hard to function without trust. To distrust people and distrust the outcomes you are seeking takes away hope and in comes fear. Fear is the ultimate drain in energy that takes over the mind and reduces life to a smaller version of all that you can and should be.

Anger, love, trust, hope, fear and faith are the foundations of our emotional needs, the emotions that come through when your values in life have over extended you. When these are in question, when these have been damaged, where do you go from there?

To repair many of the emotional gaps I had, and belief systems that were limiting me, I had to explore how my mind worked. I had to understand how the emotions I held that made me fear the use of my strengths (love, trust and hope) again in my life, and this led me to seek the tools for my mental wellbeing and the solutions that lay within my mind.

Mental wellbeing is personal

Our minds are complex, which is why there are so many thousands of books on it and why the professionals are called doctors. In this section I am uncovering five mental transitions I worked on. Again, like my healing discoveries, they were found in many ways, through books, videos, my Earth Angels and from the professionals.

If any of these trigger a thought for you, great. As before, become aware and take courage from the fact that they are not unusual, and then find your personal way to discover their impact on you and how best to heal them.

My five mental transitions

These five transitions have been invaluable to me:

1. Overdone strengths are personal

2. Values are personal

3. Boundaries are personal

4. Protection

5. Anxiety

1.   Overdone strengths are personal

Regardless of our personality type, we all have strengths. However, when our strengths are overdone or misapplied they can become weaknesses. When this happens, it can result in the emotional stress of negative emotions. I am referring here to Elias H Porter and his Relationship Awareness Theory.

In business, a major factor in our success will be the way we manage relationships with others. Porter was interested in the self-actualising aspect of human needs (Maslow's fifth and highest need), 'how we can achieve our full human potential'.

When our strengths are overdone

The following four examples have been chosen to indicate the way four personality types can overdo their strengths.

1. Those who like to help – if you are someone who likes to help others and you do this to such an extent that you neglect yourself and your own needs, this can result in emotional stress.

2. Those who strive for success – if you are someone who strives for and focuses on personal success above all else and ignores the feelings of others, this may result in failure, which will cause great distress.

3. Those who are very detailed and thorough – if you are someone who is very thorough and analytical and detailed and ignore the need to take action, you will not achieve your goals and this will cause disappointment.

4. Those who seek new and exciting things – if you are someone who likes to be creative and find new ways of doing things, but neglect the detail, execution and completion, your business is unlikely to be successful and this will result in frustration.

Emotions and behavioural change

When we find ourselves in situations that make us unhappy, and we decide to make a change, there is a tendency to go from one extreme to another. For me, my strengths of trust, hope and love became mistrust, hopelessness, fear and anger. This displayed itself as a level of assertive behaviour, dominance and a need for control in all situations. I stopped trusting in people, I let go of hope and my mind became dominated by fear and anger. There was no way to hide this. I'm sure many meetings and opportunities were destroyed by this new behaviour. It is so important when you notice these new extreme behaviours that you work to find a balance rather than gravitate towards the opposite extreme of who you are. To reset myself, I pressed pause.

At these times, you need to retreat, reflect and become more self-aware. Belief and awareness of the strengths in your personality needs to be restored in order to find yourself again. Surrounding yourself with people who have your best interests at heart and your own circle of Earth Angels will restore you. Avoiding time with people who make you feel small and bring out these shifts in your behaviour is also a great strategy. I know that once you recover yourself you will be able to manage them again.

I also made a decision to reduce my social media time. But I did maintain my community on Facebook where I felt safe. It is a place where I have encouraged honest discussions about the emotional aspect of owning a business.

It is okay to retreat – for a little while

Many of the clients I have spent time with have chosen at some time to retreat and have become introverted, removing themselves from others for fear of rejection and further pain. This is okay for a short while, but we must be aware that too long in the wilderness can create loneliness and impact one's inner drive and motivation.

This happened to me for sure. As someone who was energised by people, it was not long before my mojo left me. I accepted this and knew that when I got my strength again, when I could trust myself again, I would be back. We can always get ourselves back because the pendulum will swing back and you will be the best you, without the overdone side of your strengths. It just takes time.

2. Values are personal

I think most of us understand how we have values in our lives that can guide our intentions and beliefs. Not everyone will share the same values as you, and that is fine.

Values are personal and are often created during childhood. They can impact our belief systems. At a certain time in our lives we will all rethink our values to see if we are living the life that is true to our own values. We will ask ourselves: "Is my life turning out the way I hoped it would? Do I feel comfortable with the way I am living it?"

Value categories

Values are made up of a number of life categories that we can rate in priority to see if the reality and quality of our lives are reflected through the values we hold. For example, if you rated your health as a top three priority, giving it a seven out of 10, and then you rated your reality and it was a four out of 10, you would see the conflict in your life. Likewise, if family is a top two priority but was being treated as your seventh most important in reality, you would feel that same conflict.

I have seen a huge variety of words that can be chosen to find your core values. They usually centre around relationships, health, money, education, community interaction and social relationships.

I think they show up mostly when something is not right: when you feel life is not flowing, when you don't feel fulfilled in some way.

My values were guiding me

I spent many years feeling as if I had failed and that success was out of my reach. I had never really considered my values as being a subconscious guide in my life. A significant part of this acknowledgement of my past and my acceptance of it came when I could celebrate my family. In 2017 I had a grownup family who were balanced, happy, lovable, likeable and had a contribution to make to the world. Seeing them gain their wings and feeling the closeness of my family, despite the distance of miles, gave me a validation that I had spent 25 years of my life doing the right thing for the number one value in my life, my family.

The conflict for us all is that families cost money and so we have to chase the money and achieve a level of financial success. In Maslow's terms, this equates to the level one of physical needs that must be met for the family to survive. We get caught up in the money dream of wanting more and more. We can find ourselves measuring our success against others, and at a higher level than we really need, a higher level than our true values desire. Success can be right under our nose, we just have to be aware of our values and acknowledge them.

Not knowing your values can allow others to control you

My values conflict also showed up when I realised that I was being too flexible towards far too many people, because I valued kindness. By not having clarity around my values and how I needed to use them, I was allowing others to exploit and dominate my life. My life felt out of alignment and out of control. I soon realised the connection between values and knowing our own personal boundaries and how to protect what was right for me.

Your values and your business

A fabulous entrepreneur I have been privileged to get to know is Merlie Calvert, the founder of Farillio www.farill.io. Merlie's mission is to bring legal support to startups and small businesses. It is a platform that is growing fast and delivers access to the kind of legal advice we all need through a monthly subscription. Merlie's values shine in the way she leads and communicates her business, and they define the experience of being a client.

We meet regularly as business friends, and I asked her recently to share her values with me. I think this is enlightening and inspiring. What is perfect is that they are totally reflected in who she is as a person.

1. Empowerment – the first and foremost value of everyone in our community, team, customers, suppliers and fans.

2. Upfront and personal – no frills, no nonsense or vanity, and absolutely about the people we serve, in the trenches alongside them, not remote or preachy from a theorist's position.

3. Togetherness – truly collaborating, showcasing others and solving real problems together; recognising that we are only the wrapping around our brands that deserve recognition for who they are and what they do.

4. Tomorrow-focused – accepting the status quo is not an option. Better is a constant goal, not an end position.

Connected values – matching your personal values to your business

One of the biggest decisions you make in business is who you will work with – the team you build around your business in order to achieve the dream you have for it. Having a set of values in the way Merlie does is critical to attracting the right employees, suppliers, shareholders and partners.

If freedom is one of your values, then consider how this impacts your leadership. If success is a value, then define it and help others to buy into your definition of success. Success to them might be time. They might feel that if I work hard, I can work from home on a Friday. It might mean I get a bonus. Business leadership is about ensuring everyone is aligned in their expectations and values and can then focus on the work rather than being conflicted in the culture of the organisation.

An exercise in discovering your values is so worthwhile. There are experts in this and there is much written about it online. Reach out and discover your values and score your priorities against your reality. See the conflict in any of them and seek to solve them or accept them.

3. Boundaries are personal

At the core of my learning – and shared with me by Lis Cashin, a great friend and mental health coach – is to understand that we all have to know our boundaries. Linked to what Ruth taught me about anger, we must know when we need to protect ourselves. A time to really notice this is when your core values, your own choices in life, are being dominated by someone else. When you feel out of control.

I have tried to Google and learn how to build my boundaries as I was desperate to seek the skills to build my wall. The reality is that boundaries are personal to you. We create them just by being aware of all the things that are right for us and those that are not. Boundaries are made when you love yourself, know yourself and protect yourself. You have to learn to sense the triggers that make you feel that someone is stepping across your invisible wall – that boundary that keeps you safe.

You will feel the footsteps climbing over your wall

Our emotional state gives us a good indicator of whether or not someone has overstepped your boundary. If they made you feel dominated, out of control and uncomfortable, then the chances are that you have allowed them to begin the process of penetrating your invisible boundary. You have to know whether this is good or bad for you. Of course, sometimes we learn and grow when we are pushed a little. So, we can never assume we are always right. The best way to remain in control is to take time to consider the proposition and never feel that you can't ask for time to consider. If someone is rushing you, then they are seeking control. They have their agenda and they are not respecting you enough.

If, after reflection of a proposal that you have considered, it still feels right and you can see this new thinking from the other person is a positive learning experience for you, then take it on. Remember to acknowledge and accept that you might be out of your comfort zone but remain in control. Alternatively, if you cannot open your boundary, if it feels unsafe, then allow yourself to positively surrender. That way, you can manage the conflict with dignity and open communication and say no thank you.

4. Protection

Much of this chapter has been about how to know yourself better. At times we find ourselves in situations that we cannot be in control of – the social media world is one of them. As we build our brand, share our opinions and become known, we have to accept that not everyone will agree with us or like us.

The online world can be incredibly cruel. I have been contacted by hundreds of people who are being trolled online. This is a very damaging experience and maintaining your resilience to this can be hard. It would be ridiculous to assume that all people can cope with this. Often, individuals will think it is okay to say nasty, unwarranted things to someone they don't know, mostly with an untraceable profile because they are too weak to reveal their own identity.

High profile people get this a great deal. Sadly, so can the rest of us. The odd isolated negative comment is painful. An ongoing, relentless pursuit to damage a person is absolutely hideous. I know a number of people who have retreated from the online world due to the fear of opening their social networking doors, unsure of what they will face as a result. Consider Tracey Carr and her story of how the shareholder broke her through relentless online abuse.

All abuse is personal

Saying that you shouldn't take the abuse personally would be a reverse of what I am saying throughout this book. I believe everything is personal, as everything feels personal. Blocking this by ignoring the abusers takes a huge degree of willpower, while actually being able to stop thinking about them is virtually impossible. They are there and, for whatever reason, they have decided to target you. It could be jealousy, a feeling of injustice or it could just be a mob of people who think it is fun to target you.

I say that it is personal. However, it is unlikely to be warranted. We must realise that mental illness exists online just as it does offline, and I know from personal experience of trolls, and from hiring corporate psychologists, that some people enjoy sitting in their small lives trying to diminish any success or courage that another person shows. This was described to me as a magnet – negative is attracted to positive and once they hook on, they cannot remove themselves. There is something about someone who is doing well and is happy that attracts those who are not.

You can block these people. I found it hard to do this, but it is no different from stopping them from entering your house and abusing you, then letting them in again and again. You have to protect your energy and not allow anyone to steal it. They have no right to your attention, your content or your heart and mind. They certainly have no right to your knowledge and connections.

Are you a radiator or drain?

'Radiators and drains' is a well used phrase. Some people warm us, others make us feel drained. They literally drain us. A starting point is to look at yourself and see whether your own communication style, on and offline, is positive. Do you warm or exhaust people?

Complaining and criticising makes you a drain. I never feel the online world should be a place to complain. Only very occasionally, and as the last straw, will I go to Twitter to get the attention of a brand if I need help. As soon as we start putting negative energy into the frequency of the online world, we will begin to bond with other negative people, and we attract more negativity. Our brand will ooze negativity. A habit can form, and it becomes all too easy to start talking negatively to individuals. Our tribe, once formed, will be part of a group online that others avoid. The best way to protect yourself is to be a good person online.

The next step to give you strength is to remember the mantra: 'there are no statues to the critics'.

Trolls

Serious trolling is something very different. All online abuse falls somewhere on a spectrum, from the isolated comment that makes you feel a bit down, to the constant attack from someone or a group of people who decide to make your life hell. I write from experience as we witnessed the way 17 people behaved when we decided to ban them from our business community in 2009: Thomas and I were bombarded with hatred. Now, I am glad we experienced this as it gives me an insight into the gut-wrenching pain this creates. The ideal would be to remove oneself and go and live in a world where your digital footprint was not important, but few of us can make a living without an online presence, so this option wasn't open to us.

You can seek legal protection

We were the first people to my knowledge to experience online abuse at the level we did – the lies they spread, the destruction to our livelihood that followed. When we went to the police, they were sympathetic but laws had not been created then, so we had no legal recourse. Things are different now: there are laws, you are protected and you must use your legal rights.

For us, we had to focus on our own emotional and mental protection. Much of our sanity remained from having our own closed community around us who believed in us and knew the truth. When we needed a boost, they were there to support us. It also came from our own inner drive to continue on our quest to build good, ethical online communication.

I found a symbolic way to protect myself

My cloak

When we were under severe attack, I was given a tool which I still use – it came from a hypnotherapist. Under hypnosis, she talked me through the situation I was in and then asked me to protect myself. Under the influence of hypnosis, I could see myself in a large room, surrounded by good and bad people. Across the room was a large floor to ceiling window. I grabbed a purple velvet curtain and pulled it down, wrapping it around myself like a cloak. I would open the cloak when I was in the company of good people with good energy, but close it when I was around bad energy. To this day, I can visualise this cloak and use it when I need to.

Flicking the web of hatred off me

Another form of counter protection for me was reading about a tribe in Africa. The witch doctor could see webs formed on people and these webs were created over a lifetime of interactions with others. He could see that some were good webs that could remain stuck to the person, while other webs needed removing. He would firmly stroke the web away from the part of the body it was attached to. I have loved this ever since. When an online or offline interaction happens that is bad energy, you will see me flick away a web!

5. Anxiety

This is a very big topic. Once again, as your torchbearer, I am not going to be your expert as I can only speak from my experience of this and the aspects of knowledge that helped me. I don't think I suffered clinical anxiety. I witnessed this in others during a group therapy session and their outward symptoms often limited their lives in some way, from panic attacks to sweating and the fear of leaving their homes. My admiration for such people who overcome these life-limiting impacts is enormous. They found a way to work through their issues towards a cure.

My own experience was that I felt high levels of anxiousness at times, and I had to manage this so it didn't tip into anxiety. I would wake with a shudder, something akin to the feeling of having narrowly avoided a car accident. To overcome this, I would become active as quickly as I could and focus on routines that would calm me. Yoga, mindfulness and healing cards were my most helpful routines.

Anxiety and alcohol

I am a low-level drinker. I can take it or leave it. I never get drunk or out of control and for this reason, I never considered the link between my anxiety and alcohol. When I was coming to the end of writing this book, I realised that the occasional drinks I had were definitely affecting my morning mood the next day. It was also impacting my sleep. I am talking about the very occasional gin and tonic, nothing major.

I decided to write a post in my community on Facebook about this. Within six hours, I had 35 comments from other business owners who had discovered the same pattern, and many had reduced their alcohol consumption to a minimum while some came to a total stop.

Chris Dudley is a life coach and founder of The Coach Collective, a group of coaches brought together to support individuals challenged by their mental health. He contributed to my post as a member of our community stating: "The majority of my clients that have anxiety experience increased anxiety levels for the days following alcohol."

There is a chemical reason for this that cannot be disputed. Drinking alcohol reduces the amount of serotonin in the brain. Serotonin is a neurotransmitter that helps you feel calm and happy and low levels of it are associated with increased anxiety.

This chapter has been about our emotional and mental tools. My next learning experience was about making time for change. Ultimately change requires a commitment and these are the ways I found to achieve this.

CHAPTER 7

Making Time for Change is Personal

I have placed spiritual and physical elements in the next chapter. In this chapter I am including the disciplines of time management and prioritising the important things in your business and personal life to ensure you achieve change through balance. Creating change in your life or enhancing the skills of looking after yourself is as much about the creation of habits as it is about embedding them into your day. You can rarely escape your mind and emotions, but you have to be deliberate in your physical and spiritual dedication.

You are your own boss, the boss of your life, your destiny and legacy. Nobody else can take control – you are in control. Sometimes you have to find your own motivation to go further. If you dig deeper, you can create the life you want.

Eight-step process to change

Through my own practice to create change, I thought through many techniques that I had gathered in my life. Assembling them here is a real joy as they worked for me and helped me to honour myself, achieve my balance and ensure that I created new habits in my new life that would prevent burnout.

1. Create your habits

2. Motivate change

3. Pace – considering your day ahead, or the day you have had

4. How to do the tasks you love and those you don't

5. Honouring your 'whole self' each day

6. Creating your 'whole me' planner

7. The seven-minute rule

8. Kaizen theory for personal improvement

1. Create your habits

My desire is for your spiritual and physical practice outlined in the next chapter to become a habit. Like brushing your teeth, you do this with regularity and inner unconscious desire rather than forcing the day-to-day practice like a task that bugs you. To get to this point is not an overnight shift. It takes time. Time is a commodity and many of us have to learn how to use it in a kinder way for ourselves.

The wise words that follow, and the process of learning new habits, were shared with me years ago. Whenever I teach in life, I always refer to them.

A true habit is an unconscious skill in your life – you do it as part of a routine, unconsciously doing. To begin the process of creating a habit, you need to be motivated to create change in your life and motivated to be skilled in something. I am going to use the analogy of learning to drive a car to explain how to motivate change.

2. Motivate change

I was taught a great way to explain how we learn. This applies to anyone who wants to learn a new skill or habit in their life. When you were young, years from being able to drive a car, you had no motivation to learn. You were driven from A to B by someone and you didn't look at the gears, the pedals or even how you got to your destination. This is referred to as being 'unconsciously incompetent' and your lack of skills did not worry you.

As soon as you could see the opportunity to learn to drive approach, your interest began to grow, and you applied for your provisional license, got some L-plates and found a teacher. This stage is called being 'consciously incompetent'. You now know what you don't know, but you want to learn.

Once you have been shown how to drive and you practise a lot, you stop being unconsciously incompetent and find yourself having a conscious level of competence. You have the awareness and skills to do what you need to do, but you still need to practise, practise, practise. Without daily practice you cannot form the habit. The more you practise, the more you stop thinking about how to do something, and you start to enjoy the feeling of doing it. It feels effortless.

Finally, yippee! After a lot of practice and discipline, you have become 'unconsciously competent' and the habit is formed. Using the driving analogy, you have arrived at a destination without even realising the path you took.

Applying this to your spiritual practice and your physical wellbeing, you will now want to do this habitually so it becomes part of your routine, and a new healthier you will emerge.

3. Pace – considering your day ahead, or the day you have had

My own path to learning spiritual practice and to being physically fitter gave me an insight into how I treated each day.

When I began to make a change, I witnessed in myself the habits I had in all aspects of life – it was a manic, functional rush. I believed that all actions, whether the spiritual moments or the physical, were measured by time. I placed a pressure on myself to achieve an outcome. It was just another task in my day. Then one day, I thought about the day ahead of me and I realised that I had a day of calm. I was working from home with only a couple of phone calls and no deadlines. So why was I doing my practice at the same pace? Rather than 15 minutes of commitment, I could give it half an hour. Rather than adding more to the practice, I just slowed it down. I also realised that not every day had to be the same routine. I could apply different physical and spiritual practices to my day and vary the time I gave it. I loosened the reins of controlling this part of my life so tightly.

4. How to do the tasks you love and those you don't

Many years ago, an amazing business mentor and speaker I know, Roger Hamilton, spoke on stage about 'flame' and 'wax'. We all have things we love doing in business – these are things that come naturally to us, they seem easy – our flame. Then there are those activities in our business lives that we avoid because they drain us – our wax.

If we see life as a candle, the flame in us can light a million other flames, but when we are in our wax, we drown, get tired and light few people's lives.

We have to accept that all business people need to be disciplined to do some wax tasks. Our business will thrive if we use our time well, spending the energetic time in our day to accomplish our flame tasks. We can do our wax tasks in a chunk of time that is still respectful of its importance, but it does not impact on that key time when we can be at our best.

What is your flame and wax?

To do this exercise, list all the things that sit within your business and life that feel as if they set you on fire, and all the things that drown you. You will know them as some give you energy, while the others exhaust you.

These will vary depending on your personality. You may be a people person or a task-driven person; you may be an extrovert or an introvert; are you detailed or big picture oriented? List what you are good at and what comes naturally, and also what you find hard.

We cannot expect every activity and moment in our lives to be only filled with joy and achievement. This exercise is important for you to find balance, and appreciate when you do the things that are tough, and allow the appropriate time for the things you enjoy.

Your Flame (achievement) Gives Energy	Your Wax (avoid and procrastinate) Takes Energy Away
Writing a blog	Working out tax
Meeting clients	Writing proposals
Speaking at events	Doing slides for speaking
Yoga	Business development activities
Mindfulness	
Resting in front of a good box set	

When you start to build your business, you may find a business partner who likes the things you don't enjoy, or you might find suppliers who do the tasks you want to delegate, or employ people with a job description and skills to do these things. Keep hold of your flame though. What you are good at is the best thing you bring to your business.

5. Honouring your 'whole self' each day

We all have 24 hours in a day. Time is a commodity that we can either control or be controlled by. We can choose the way our day works for us.

Fitting in our wellbeing practice and fitness around our daily demands is about choosing whether you are motivated to feel stronger for business and life, and then allocating the time to do it.

When I recognised that I was not in control of my life, I came to terms with the fact that this was as much about how I allocated time to myself as it was about the emotional and mental learning I was going through.

During a session with Anna, my psychologist, we worked on a Cognitive Behavioural Technique (CBT) referred to as Behavioural Activation, which helps to modify mood through ensuring we are doing activities that are supportive of our mood. I wanted to ensure that when I was back fully in the business world, I would not go down the same path of overwork and lack of personal consideration for my health. I also needed to stop procrastinating over some tasks.

The following four categories will help you manage your mood against the activities you need to achieve:

- The activities in life that give you a sense of accomplishment
- The activities in life that give you pleasure
- Things you tend to avoid
- Activities that are in line with your values

Begin this process by writing a list of things that sit within each category

This enables you to consider the emotions you have around things that you should do, want to do, and it allows you to prioritise yourself in your day. Looking after your wellbeing is not indulgent. You are your greatest asset in business and if you are not rested and fit, if you have not achieved the tasks in your business that have to be done, then all of this will impact your emotions and your mental state and ultimately your business will suffer.

Ensure you do something every day that respects your personal values – this is very important. We talked about values in the last chapter. If your values are health and longevity, then fitness is part of this. If they do not feature, then find somewhere in this table to place it. Accept how you feel about it and get on with getting fit and finding rest time for your soul.

6. Creating your 'whole me' planner

The following example is just a few of the things that could sit in each category in order to give you a starting point. The idea is that you should spend time writing many things in each column so that you can allocate, with balance, your time to achieve the values you hold and the habits you want to form in your life.

Once you have written your list, create a plan for each day. Ideally, try to create this in advance and allocate some of items as an appointment with yourself.

To get myself into the habit of this, I would plan my next day each evening. I created a column for each category on a pad of paper and added the plan for my day making sure I took something from each category.

Accomplishments	Pleasure	Avoid/Procrastinate	In line with your values
Write a blog	Tea in bed when I wake	Update my LinkedIn profile	Do 15 minutes of mindfulness colouring
Write proposal for client X	Invite a friend over for supper	Look at the SEO of my website	Have my father for supper
Do my accounts for the month	Have a 30-minute lunch break in front of the TV	Work out my tax	Go for a 30-minute walk

7. The seven-minute rule

When our mood is low, or we are struggling with motivation for some other reason, it can be helpful to employ what Anna referred to as the seven-minute rule. This is a helpful strategy to use when you have scheduled to do something but can't seem to get going with it. If you accept that doing the task is not optional, but your motivation is particularly low, you have to start it but have the option of stopping after seven minutes should you choose to do so. This is a successful technique because starting a task is generally the hardest part; once the task is underway, most people find that they will carry it on beyond the seven minutes.

8. Kaizen theory for personal improvement

Kaizen is a Japanese word meaning improvement. It is adopted by many organisations to foster innovation and progress. Wikipedia defines it as 'change for better' with an inherent meaning of continuous improvement.

When I was told about this by my great friend Ailsa Adkin, I applied my own take on this to my time management and sense of continual progress. I broke my day into tiny parts and listed all the activities that I achieved. I included all aspects of my life that required progress and praised myself for my continued improvement. This included my home, business and self.

The two work together. Each day I progressed and improved. Each day I became fitter, my spiritual practice improved and my business improved.

The joy of ticking off your list of achievements

To truly embrace this, I encourage you to write everything you do in a list each day. You can write it as a task list that you want to achieve, but also add in the additional things you do. The list of continual improvement will astound you. Celebrate the whole you.

Your home, your domestic achievements, your exercise – you might also add the ways you have supported others to achieve. Giving and contributing to others is the best way to raise your energy and self-esteem, because, feeling valued is priceless.

List your business achievements each day and don't just log the final tick item on a project, list every step you are taking. Your wellbeing is about you seeing that you are amazing, that even rest is an achievement, as is seeing a friend, taking time for you and spending time in your business. Celebrate it all.

Now, my hope is that you will see the next steps in this book as important. I hope you are not fearful about applying the time you need to nurture yourself so that you can achieve a strong business. I believe that when we have a strong heart, mind, soul and body, our business will be stronger.

CHAPTER 8

Spiritual Habit is Personal

Throughout this book, I want you to be the best you can be. To be emotionally strong, mentally fit, spiritually connected and physically healthy. I am restating this constantly as a reminder of the intent of the book. Our emotional and mental states are with us all the time – in our heads we are thinking, being and managing each moment we encounter. We observe and react. We feel and we think. We can rarely close off the noise in our heads. Our habit is to think.

The practice of looking after our souls is not new to thousands of entrepreneurs I witness in their online content. For years I was slightly wary of the messages they were sending out.

I know from my own slow uptake of the word 'spiritual' that many business people find it hard to consider this aspect of their whole being. I felt better when someone said that being spiritual meant I was 'looking after my soul'. The part of me that is who I am.

Half ego, half spirit

Some time ago, I read a book that talked of us being 'a spirit formed in human shape' while on earth we are half ego and half spirit. I like this a lot. We have permission to be ego. We must have ego as it allows our human shape to exist and survive. We have to find our food, build connections and have self-esteem in order to compete for food. However, when our ego becomes larger than our spirit, we are in danger of creating our stress and our unhappiness, and we get out of touch with who we are as we strive to be bigger, richer, more powerful. We could also refer to spirit as our soul. We need to nurture our soul to achieve balance.

I am not an extreme person. When I discover things, I seek to find a balanced way to live. I always believed that spiritual people had made a commitment far greater than I was willing to make.

That said, when I was very young, less than 10 years old, I remember thinking that I had a responsibility to the person who got my soul after I died. I have no idea why I had this belief. I just remember the huge responsibility to accept challenges positively, to treat people well and to endeavour to contribute to make others happy.

For me, discovering spiritual practice was random and not linked to any particular practice. When I was at school I attended chapel every Wednesday. Apart from that, and the occasional wedding, funeral or christening, I never went back to church.

People around me have shared amazing spiritual words that have moved me. Follow some Instagram profiles and you can get a daily dose of great words. I was aware that some people meditated, and I was aware of the growth in mindfulness.

Spiritual practice is more universal than expected

I want to put your mind at rest by telling you about a short workshop I ran within an all-male group of successful, professional 40 somethings – not a Millennial or Tree Hugger (excuse my deliberate stereotyping) among them. In advance of the workshop, I asked them to consider this question: What success rituals do you have? I termed it this way because I thought they might feel this was more their language for business. I was hugely surprised when, one by one, they shared their morning routine of meditation, yoga, mindfulness and how they cared for their soul on a daily basis. I seriously never imagined that about them.

Spiritual practice is personal

Some of the most serious and successful business people I know use spiritual practice as part of their daily routine. I think we all need calm moments when we can listen and allow thoughts to enter our minds that are positive, restful and loving.

What we are doing with these rituals is relaxing our tired minds and nurturing the core of who we are.

I have now learned that stilling the mind and allowing an energy to enter is very powerful. I also feel strongly that the methods you use are personal to you. I have not approached my spiritual awakening with any strategy. During my early dive into this world, I chose to have a shallow dive. I didn't read a book, attend a course or hire a practitioner. All of this would have been too overwhelming for me, but my commitment to myself was to find peace in my soul and I was very aware that spiritual practice was the best way. I had a hold on my emotions, I understood how my mind worked, the next step was to learn how to nourish my soul.

I want to share a timeline of my awakening as a case study – your torchbearer. I am calling this my awakening as I am nowhere near fully living it yet, but the small amount I do has helped me enormously as a person. It has calmed me, allowing new perspectives to form and it has made me far more creative. Ultimately, I sense it has stopped me from pushing all the time.

Additionally, my spiritual practice has given me a calmer view of the world. It provides a door that I can open and step into when I need peace, and a place to love and understand myself and find tolerance and resilience. It is definitely the way to find faith, hope and love, things I found so challenging at the beginning of my recovery. Spiritual practice is a lifelong journey with yourself, with the half of yourself that is your spirit.

You can hide inside your practice

The beauty of spiritual practice is that it is personal to you – your secret. During your spiritual time you are able to visualise and believe in your deepest desires and thoughts and never feel small, always knowing that anything is possible. I am told that in this space you give yourself, you are opening the universal channels, the energy that exists all around us that seeks to improve the world. Only lessons learned by us all, only great energy goes back into the universe, and when you are part of this, that energy will flow back to you. This is a beautiful belief that I am choosing to be part of. I am a student of this now and I am slowly, cautiously learning at my own personal pace.

The joy of being alive

My personal motivation to practise spirituality is to calm my mind, give me more peace, find my creativity and have the daily strength to deal with challenges that are inevitable. I feel this will help me be my best self and give me a longer life that is happier, not from the joy of life but more from the joy of being alive.

When I do my spiritual practice, it is my business, myself and loved ones that I think of. Each day and each practice is different. Your life and your business are so personal to you, you will have deep dreams, fears and battles to overcome, times when you are overwhelmed, and times when you are underwhelmed. Days when you have to self-start and days that have so much momentum that you wake up ready to keep working to a level of abuse of yourself that you will not feel until it brings you down. Your life deserves to be the best you can have. You can be amazing. In fact, we need you to be amazing – the world needs amazing people.

Choosing your practice

I have listed several areas that I have explored, as your torchbearer. There are many more and some deeply connected people who can teach you the practice of any that you desire.

These are the ones I have explored and discuss in more detail here:

- Affirmations
- Healing cards
- Prayer
- Church
- Yoga
- Gratitude
- Mindfulness
- Numerology

Affirmations

Ten years ago, I started to use affirmations. These affirm your desires and allow you to overcome blocks. This is a tool I use four or five times a year when I am extra challenged and need to write down a brief paragraph of something I want to happen or believe in.

The practice of affirmations is used by millions of people who have been taught positive thinking. They work for me. The belief system behind them is that when you write something in the present, believing it has happened, repeated four times a day for 28 days, your mind believes it to be true and you become the thing you have affirmed. The critical aspect of an affirmation is that you never use negative words.

When I write them, I use a hard piece of card and type them or write them out four times. I have a copy in my purse, on my bathroom cabinet, in the kitchen and anywhere else I know I will see and read them at least four times. It is a habit you have to form by doing it every day for at least 28 days. This is about reprogramming your mind.

Some would argue that this is not spiritual practice. For me, I make sure it is. All the words I choose are about my soul, my spirit and the messages I want to be part of in the universe.

Healing cards

You may have seen healing cards in bookshops, gift shops or online. They are a pack of cards, designed with pictures and words and usually created by spiritual people.

I came across these when a family member faced the most terrible challenge in her life, she was grief stricken. A friend gave her a set of fairy healing cards, and she told me they helped her. I had never seen anything like this and bought my own set. Each day I shuffled the cards, picked one out and read the little booklet that accompanied the card to see how I could interpret the card in a way that was relevant to my current challenges. There was always a positive statement that I could interpret and enjoy.

The biggest thing I learned from this was the joy of sitting still for a few moments at the start of my day and going through this routine. It gave me a moment of calm. I don't use them every day, but I do reach for them when I need an extra boost of inspiration and belief in the world and to find my faith again.

Prayer in groups or alone

When I felt loneliness during the time I was healing, I found I wanted to belong to a social group in my town where the members cared for one another. I didn't want to take all my pain to my husband, close friends and my children. I liked the idea of a group of people with whom I could meet every week. We could share discoveries, joys and challenges. I wanted to hear their stories, their lives and to help others. So, I went online and Googled 'Prayer Groups'. I couldn't find one in my town. My mother-in-law has belonged to one for years and I have seen the amazing way they support one another. I think these are beautiful groups.

I think there is an opportunity for multi-faith groups to come together to listen to one another's challenges. If there is one in your town, I suggest you take a peep and try one out. If there isn't one, perhaps this would be an amazing group to create.

Prayer is also a great comfort to many, and I have learned to adopt this and am on a journey to understand more. I pray in gratitude as there is always something to be grateful for. Sometimes I just give thanks for the fact I am strong enough to deal with the challenges I face. I use prayer to pray for others. The energy I focus on is to feel a connection to something greater than anything I can see. I seek to nurture my faith, the faith that no matter what life is throwing at me, it will pass, that I will learn and my life will find the right path.

Church

The week that I Googled 'Prayer Groups' created an interesting, serendipitous experience and a new spiritual practice for me.

I was walking through a supermarket in my local town when I bumped into Mary Haines. We had crossed paths as mums for over 20 years, casual acquaintances at our children's swimming lessons or on the touchline of a rugby match. As we chatted, I discovered that she was an active member of the church near where I live and I mentioned that I wanted to join a prayer group. She said she wasn't aware of one, but invited me to join her at church that Sunday.

I was hesitant that Sunday morning. It felt strange to me – I wasn't seeking God. I was seeking a loving place, a happy place and somewhere that I would feel connected that wasn't about business. I knew that the more I found inner happiness and calm, the more I would grow, and the business would flourish from this new energy and balance. I felt uncomfortable about entering church though, as I wasn't a strong believer.

Modern church, I have discovered, is not just about worship, although I have come to enjoy that. The perception from my childhood was that I would be beaten down with the doom of hell and guilt. The reality was that I heard and felt faith, hope and love, and this incredible community of people also shared an energy towards one another – the hugs, the smiles and the togetherness. It was a place to matter, to care and be cared for. (I only know the Christian faith, although I am very interested in all faiths.)

My weekly visit to church gives me faith. A faith in people. It gives me a time to reflect, a calm time to connect into a higher source of energy. It is a very beautiful 90 minutes in my week.

These are the words of my favourite hymn, which I have on my Spotify Playlist so I can ensure I hear them several times a week. Surely they apply to any of us as a set of values to follow and give us faith in others? These help me to focus outwards and ensure that, despite my own needs in life, I continue to care for others.

Make me a channel of your peace

Where there is hatred let me bring your love

Where there is injury, your pardon Lord

And where there's doubt, true faith in you

Make me a channel of your peace

Where there's despair in life let me bring hope

Where there is darkness, only light

And where there's sadness ever joy

Oh, master grant that I may never seek

So much to be consoled as to console

To be understood as to understand

To be loved as to love with all my soul

Make me a channel of your peace

It is in pardoning that we are pardoned

In giving to all men that we receive

And in dying that we're born to eternal life

Yoga

My New Year resolution was to learn yoga. I wanted to be good at one part of it, specifically the Sun Salutations with Downward Dog. I learned that this one practice exercises every muscle. I know that millions of people go to yoga classes every week. I can see the attraction. The balance of mind and body is so inspiring, and its impact is clearly powerful.

I hired Cathy Richardson, a yoga teacher, to come to my house for an hour a week for eight weeks. I learned the correct form from a professional and understood my body and how it moved. There are so many YouTube channels you can follow, but I think you need to see a teacher first, either one to one or in a class to ensure you are getting it right. The movements are very precise.

I mentioned earlier that I am not someone who adopts things in a full-on way. My daily 15–30 minutes of yoga in the garden if it's a good day, or in the house on a wet day, is enough for me and it is manageable. Adopting it in this way enables it to be part of my daily spiritual practice and I combine it with either affirmations or healing cards plus a short period of mindfulness and gratitude.

I have created a special space for this where I have a small Buddha statue from Bali that my daughter gave me, a mat and a candle. I always do six repeats of the movement, either fast or slow, depending on the pace I have set for my day.

Gratitude

I always apply gratitude throughout the yoga practice. I find it incredibly important in this practice to be grateful, rather than needing. I was so inspired when I read the book *Tuesdays with Morrie* by Mitch Albom. In the book, Morrie, who is dying of a nervous disease, always celebrates the parts of his body he has left, not the parts he has lost. If we can be grateful rather than 'wanting' all the time, I think we experience a much better filter on life.

I would suggest you adopt gratitude as the first change you make. Consider the continual progress you make each day, the people you come into contact with, the love of others, even the fact that you have food to eat. We should take nothing for granted.

Mindfulness

I first came across the concept of mindfulness years ago in the form of colouring books. I am aware that the practice of mindfulness is spreading rapidly and is being used to manage anxiety and depression by some wellness specialists including psychologists. I find this a way to take my mind off life's issues and the constant desire to solve everything. When we do this, it requires little mental energy and we give our minds a rest.

Breath and the art of mindful breathing is the place to start. We breathe all the time of course, but this is the art of noticing and focusing on your breath. It is not about breathing differently, but rather about experiencing your breath without changing it, just focusing on it by blocking out all other thoughts and actions. You can still notice the sounds and the textures of what you have around you: the birds, traffic, voices, the texture of the material your hands are resting on. Work your way around your body in the now, noticing everything. By being still and allowing yourself to think, you take your mind off the past and the future and you rest in the thoughts they fill you with. I find this is a type of distraction from the world, because in this moment I am at peace and resting and allowing universal energy to flow in and out of me.

A have met many people who find running, gardening, colouring useful, basically any task that enables them to connect with the present and stop regretting the past or worrying about the future. All we have is now. Living in the present is a wonderful, restful thing to do. It is the ultimate feeling of faith and letting go.

The most common way to describe this is that you notice the simple things in life, and you are very present, distracting your mind by focusing and thinking of the actions you are taking. The example so often used is of washing hands. When you wash your hands, do it with deliberate thought, notice the tap, turn it on, notice how easy or hard it is to turn, see the water gush out, appreciate the ease of water in your life, put soap on your hands, smell it, feel it, and feel the water wash it off, turn the tap off, dry your hands, noticing the towel texture. For that short moment you are relaxing your mind, just like allowing your leg muscles to relax after a run. Nothing should be 'on' all the time. We seek to solve problems and race around our heads all the time.

There are so many apps available for mindfulness. Headspace and Calm are two I have subscribed to.

Practise, practise, practise – it is the only way for you to believe the impact it will have on you. This practice has helped me in times of stress, and I have found I have greater faith in myself and the future, and a greater ability to live in the now when challenges hit me. Where I used to go straight to fear about my future, I now remind myself of the actual moment I am in and the safety of it.

I guess in this mad, mad world, we are seeking more, expecting more and being more. We try to constantly solve our problems, thinking about the past, planning our future. If we can adopt ways to be in the moment we strengthen our minds, something that has been scientifically proven.

If being in the present interests you more, may I suggest you read *The Power of Now* by Eckhart Tolle. This quote is a very powerful one from him:

"As soon as you honour the present moment, all unhappiness and struggle dissolve, and life begins to flow with joy and ease. When you act out the present moment awareness, whatever you do becomes imbued with a sense of quality, care and love – even in the most simple action."

Finally, numerology

I like fun moments in my day that are triggered by numbers. For me, numerology is a great way of getting a message from the universe and weirdly the messages are so often right. The number 1111 appears so many times in front of me on a clock and I always send them to my son Ross and to a great friend in New Zealand. The number 444 seems to be a time I regularly wake. If this intrigues you, if you like the thought of a spiritual prompt in your day, you can look the numbers up online. Google the number you have seen with regularity, adding the word 'numerology'.

Your personal spiritual practice and your business

It is important to find time for your soul when you are in business. I read posts online from business people every day that indicate stress, fear and desperation. Owning a business and having ambition demands a lot of the whole you. Spiritual practice gives you a way to manage the inner you, your soul. Your soul is who you are, and your emotions and your mental state can impact your soul. My spiritual practice helps me counterbalance my emotions and mind.

When you look after your soul it will bring balance and enables you to be a better business person, a more balanced and considered person with an energy that enables you to listen better, protect yourself better and contribute better. When the soul is neglected we have all the emotions of fear, anger and defence. None of these are attractive to the business world.

Your practice is personal, so create your plan and start to experiment with what works for you. It is important that it is enjoyable, enriching and achieves an emotional and mental calmness. If your practice increases your stress, then it is not right for you.

I have only touched on the need for this and the path I am taking. Now you should decide if this would assist you and create a plan to discover your personal spiritual practice.

CHAPTER 9

Your Physical Wellbeing is Personal

Longevity

The chances are many of us could live to be 100 years old. The statistics on average ages are extending and while some of us will suffer diseases and accidents, the reality is that many of us will extend our lives through our self-awareness and through the amazing advancements in medicine. This is a joy for us all, but there is a caveat: it is a joy providing we can do it with health and not just because the medics won't allow us to die.

The other reality of a longer life means we have to work longer to ensure we can fund the lifestyle we seek. Finding the motivation to look after our physical wellbeing is not an option for any of us.

Our mind and body

We cannot ignore the impact the mind has over our physical health. The link between stress and our health is hard to argue against. We also know the impact that physical health has on our minds – the powerful endorphins that create joy and positivity and rid our bodies of stress hormones.

We also all know the moment when we feel a physical manifestation of something that doesn't feel right to us. The fear or anger that we suddenly feel when we are under attack, when the body is saying protect yourself. From Ruby Wax's TED Talk I mentioned earlier, in primitive times this was a clear danger we were reacting to. Now most of our stress hormones are created through modern communication and expectations.

The biochemical impact of mental stress

The physical reaction we have when our mind becomes preoccupied by a bad feeling is a biochemical one. I attended a lecture and wrote these words down that were shared by a panel of experts who listed the chain of reactions when stress hits us.

1. The brain sends a message to your pituitary gland and this encourages your adrenal gland to release adrenalin.

2. You might get a physical reaction at this point such as a dry mouth, a dizzy feeling, even a feeling of deliberate swallowing.

3. At this point your breathing may increase. This is to send more oxygen to your muscles, exactly for the reason of 'get ready to run'.

4. Your heart will pump faster, your blood pressure may rise.

   Your body says, 'I need more energy' and as if by magic, your liver releases stored sugar, so you can run fast and long. Of course, it is rare that you are actually going to use this increase of sugar, rarely will you actually run. More likely, you are sitting in a room with someone, or at your laptop.

5. When you have excess unused sugar in your body, you may get indigestion.

6. The adrenalin in your system causes blood to be diverted from your stomach to other organs, so digestion slows down.

7. This can cause nausea and ulcers.

If we continue to have these experiences many times in our working lives, we can see why our bodies start to be under attack.

We cannot stop the modern world, nor can we control the way things happen and the way people behave. The only thing we can do is take control of our own self and our health. This book, so far, has been about reducing these moments of stress by knowing what is right for you, your values and your personal choices, by taking away the strain of being like others and just being yourself. Encouraging you to create a business that is personal to you and your choices.

The other thing we can do to stay strong is to exercise.

Taken from content on the Anxiety and Depression Association of America (ADAA), this statement and statistics about how Americans manage stress is helpful to validate my desire for you:

> *"It's impossible to eliminate, but you can learn to manage stress, and most people usually do. According to a recent ADAA online poll, some 14 percent of people make use of regular exercise to cope with stress. Others reported talking to friends or family (18 percent); sleeping (17 percent); watching movies or TV (14 percent), as well as eating (14 percent) and listening to music (13 percent).*
>
> *While all of these are well-known coping techniques, exercise may be the one most recommended by health care professionals. And among ADAA poll takers who exercise, a healthy percentage is already on the*

right track: walking (29 percent), running (20 percent), and yoga (11 percent) are their preferred strategies.

They go on to state that "exercise and other physical activity produce endorphins, chemicals in the brain that act as a natural painkiller, and also improve the ability to sleep, which in turn reduces stress."

Your choice of physical health is personal to you

Let's accept that we do live in such a full-on world. All around us are images of beautiful bodies, the gym lovers, the constant confronting reminders that we should be keeping fit. I have found this overwhelming and not at all motivating. I cannot motivate my fitness by vanity. I want to grow my inner beauty more than my outer. What will motivate your increased physical activity is personal to you.

Exercise is also mindfulness

I have been on a cross-trainer or running machine when a blast of creativity floods in when I was least expecting it, when I was not trying to solve a problem. Music in my ear, counting down time or repetitions, I have stilled my conscious mind and in doing so, my unconscious mind has thrown me a lifeline, a solution or an idea. Many runners, swimmers and gym enthusiasts tell me this is normal for them.

No one has time for fitness, so get past that excuse

When we spiral into overworking and exhaustion, we may have occasional feelings of anxiety or low moods. This is when we are not always able to give our best selves to the business. The last thing we feel we can fit into our lives is to add yet more to our day. We convince ourselves that we need rest, sleep and time in front of the TV. Bringing up children, managing a business, running a household – I know how keeping fit can be the last thing on our minds. I always assumed those who kept fit must have less to do than I have, and they must have more time in their lives. The reality is that they knew to prioritise their fitness in order to be a great parent, great business person, and a great person in general.

I want to add that even the fittest people I know have to push themselves out of the door. I was so relieved when my fittest friend said she hated the build-up to going for a run. I always assumed I had to love it. So again, that is a myth you can use as an excuse, but it is not valid.

I apply the rules I set out in Chapter 7: Making Time for Change is Personal, to my exercise regime. Little by little, the seven-minute rule has become longer, and the activity has shifted from avoid to achieve.

Making health your addiction

As soon as we make physical wellbeing a priority, we can adopt a wide view of how we can achieve it. Starting our day by choosing the foods and patterns of eating that feel right for us is important. We need to ensure we have allocated time for some physical activity each day, while ensuring our choices are not too extreme for us to manage for the rest of our lives. Very soon these habits become more addictive than the lifestyle we have left behind.

When emotional wellbeing manifests physical problems

During my period of emotional and mental awakening, I became aware of the ways I have locked anger down, blocked out emotions of failure and experienced a lack of respect from people who were communicating with me in a way I should not have tolerated. I believed I was resilient to the way my life was throwing me challenges.

This spread into my physical resilience. For many years I suffered a constant pain in my stomach. I put it down to acid and indigestion, which of course was probably true. Eventually, when the pain started to worry my family, I went to see a specialist. Two weeks later, my gall bladder was removed. It was inflamed and had the appearance of many infections. There were no stones, just lots of grit, which clearly caused pain as it flowed into my system.

Six days after the operation, I was due on stage as a speaker at an event. Worried by my recovery and the heavy anaesthetic and painkillers, I arranged to see a reiki practitioner, Anusha, to help me sleep and recover. As I sat with her, she asked me about my life and I shared some of the trials, losses and stresses. She wrote the words down. Then I explained that I was recovering from a gall bladder removal five days earlier. Pulling a book down from her bookcase, Anusha showed me a page that broke the body down into various sections and applied the emotional issues that could cause gall bladder problems. The three emotional words linked to failing gall bladders were 'the emotion of anger, fear of failure and the need for respect'.

I have now learned that the physical manifestations of our lives can often be the last message our minds can give us to make us take action. When our emotions have been ignored, when we carry unresolved mental anguish and we have ignored our spiritual wellbeing, our bodies will cry out.

We are very fortunate if the physical manifestation is curable, as it was in my case. If there was ever a moment in my life when the dots joined up and I learned the link between all four elements that make us whole, this was it.

Fitness is personal

Choosing your route to fitness is your choice. However, you must find it. Respecting your body and building a healthy level of physical exertion into your life is not a choice if you want to live a long and healthy life.

Set your own goals

Whether you want to run a marathon, lose several pounds, lift heavier weights, feel more attractive, live longer or just get rid of your nagging feeling, make a decision to do it. Don't avoid it as your business needs you to be healthy and fit. The mental impact is the greatest aspect of exercise as it lifts your mood. I began to love exercise when I felt the mental benefits far more than the physical change.

My church of endorphins

I have discussed the routine I have for church on a Sunday, but I have another church, which I call my church of endorphins, or my weekly commitment to exercise. I chose to hire a personal trainer, Suzanne O'Callaghan from Lifestyle Fitness. I meet her once a week on a Monday at 9am. It is fabulous to start my week like this as it energises my mind and body for the work ahead. I could do this on my own, but I want to keep having a fixed appointment with someone who pushes me harder than I would push myself. I use my two practices of church and gym every week to allow me to release and acknowledge any stress or sadness.

I wrote at the start of this chapter about the impact that stress can have on our physical health. We cannot avoid stress, but we can create a way to remove those toxins we create. I have found this invaluable. I also love the endorphins, now my little friends, that run around my body and make me feel joyful.

Put it in your planner

If you have decided to add physical health to your plan, then make a plan and set yourself a goal. Put it in your 'whole me' day planner. Tag it as you feel it – avoid, achieve, pleasure or in line with your values – but do it. You will feel amazing and it won't be long before exercise becomes an unconscious competency in your life, when habit takes over and you cannot imagine a life without this new energy.

Nutrition is personal

I am not a fan of diets that are extreme in their results (assuming that sudden weight loss is not medically required). An attitude to lifelong fitness and health is best. I am not slim, I am not fat, I have curves. I don't have defined muscle structure. What I focus on is stamina and energy and to know that my mind feels energised. Critically, I no longer have the nagging worry that I am abusing my body. I tend to eat healthily, but if I want to have the occasional treat, I do this without guilt. Again, this is personal to me and is the balance I seek. I am managing my health rather than trying to win any prizes.

Sugar, fats, salt, crisps, sweets, chips, fast food – the explosion of this in our lives does not need to be written about in detail here. We all know these things are bad for us. They are addictive and they are dangerous. They also have a horrible impact on our energy and vitality.

When I eat sugar now, I need to sleep. If I eat fatty food, I feel sluggish. Once we remove these foods from our diet we notice their impact so acutely when we treat ourselves to something naughty. This alone has made me really appreciate the joy of healthy eating. I was never very bad, but I was never really good either.

We all have different constitutions, which is why one way of eating works for some and not others. Apart from personal choice in the types of food we eat, we also need to know what times of the day work best so we understand what energises us and what exhausts us. Carbohydrates make me so exhausted, whereas to another person they are a critical part of their diet.

I choose not to eat meat but I do eat fish, while some people are vegans. The varied ways we now eat are written up and shared across the social media networks and we are not short of advice if we want it. The challenge comes from the overwhelming choices and opinions. Add to that the industry of vitamins and protein products and this is a very confusing world.

I have always applied the fairly basic knowledge that I need to expend more calories than I eat in a day. It makes sense to me that if I work at home on my laptop and move only from my office to the kitchen, I must make sure I eat fewer calories. Those days when I have four appointments in London followed by a speech in the evening demands that my calories are higher. It is not rocket science.

The complex part is knowing how efficient we are at consuming and digesting our foods, knowing what our bodies like and dislike and using our common sense through considering how we feel after a meal.

Intermittent fasting

Many people believe in the process of intermittent fasting. This is creating a pattern of eating in your life that means you fast for 16–18 hours of the day. It is not a new idea and has been used throughout history. I know many people who are applying this to their lives and are experiencing many benefits in the form of energy and weight loss. My son Ross, aged 23 when he began, has been practising this for over a year and feels fantastic. He says his mind is more alert, his body is more toned and his energy is greater than ever before. He does not eat before 2pm and will ensure all his eating is done before 8pm. If he is going out for a later dinner, then he will start eating later in the day.

Skipping breakfast laughs in the face of the marketing that the breakfast companies did for years, stating that 'breakfast is the most important meal of the day'. I guess it might be for some, but again, finding your own personal path to great nutritional habits is where you will benefit most.

Monitoring your health and getting advice

We cannot ignore our nutritional needs. What we put into our bodies is without doubt going to impact our performance, concentration and productivity in business. I chose to have blood tests on a quarterly basis with a company that sends a kit to my house https://thriva.co and gives me a reading in a report several days later. I also got the advice from a professional nutritionist when I needed it. I honour the skills of others and if their knowledge helps me to eat the right food for me, then I think it is worth investing in.

Vitamins

The vitamins industry is growing year on year. In 2015, the UK generated £414 million of revenue for the vitamin companies, reporting that 65% of all adults reported taking some form of supplement every day. (Source: Mintel Reports: Vitamins and Supplements – UK, Sept 2016.) Ensuring that you buy regulated and well-produced vitamins is essential. I now have a subscription for vitamins and they are sent to my house every month. This ensures I take the vitamins that balance my health, combat cyclical deficiencies such as vitamin D and boost my immune system. I know that the best chance of defending myself against cancer is a strong immune system. I have my nephew Alexander Eastman to thank for introducing me to the importance of vitamins from the enormous amounts of research he undertook with such dedication since he lost his sister, my beautiful niece Vicki, to cancer.

If you have read this section and feel it resonates, consider creating your 'whole being food plan':

- Create a list of what you know is bad for you that you should remove over time.

- Create a list of the things you would like to introduce into your diet that you know would be good for you.

- Notice how food makes you feel.

- Have your blood analysed for any deficiencies.

- Consider the pattern of eating that suits you and works well in your business life.

- Take control and don't just reach for food when you are hungry. We all choose the fast energy food when we are like this and these can be the most damaging.

Up to this point in the book I have focused on the way to create a strong emotional, mental, spiritual and physical life and, in doing this, create a strong business that you and others can thrive from.

Next, we will look at how important it is to value yourself in the business world, ensure you have the basic skills required in business and how to be in the connected world that we have created together, as it shifts and turns, ensuring you remain relevant and deeply connected.

CHAPTER 10

The Value You Place on Yourself is Personal

The subject of appreciating the value you have to others is very important when you are in business. Whether working for yourself or employed, your time, emotion and the skills you bring to your working practices are unique to you.

The fourth layer of Maslow's five basic human needs is esteem, the need to have recognition and the respect of others. This may sound ego driven, and it is. Ego is a survival mechanism, and although it needs to be controlled, it is still a critical need for your motivation and business survival.

In business, the ultimate measurement of being valued is the achievement of fees and income. For some, being helpful and kind is a high value, however, the exchange of money for the contribution you make to your client is the only way your business can grow and you can thrive. Without the sense of being valued, all humans are in danger of sinking into low self-esteem.

The consequences of being undervalued can be challenging. Some people will overcompensate and seek to overbuild their brand and focus too much on the respect of others rather than on their business. Seeking praise, attention and making a noise, we all see a lot of this online.

Before we move on to Chapter 11, where I share some of the processes and skills that will help you, I want to share the risks of not calculating and trusting in your value.

How you treat yourself will determine the culture of your business

A fundamental aspect of starting and running a business is that it should serve you. It should pay you, love you, honour you and be you. Your leadership will determine the way others see your business whether you are a sole trader or leading a large company. The way your business treats you and others connected with it will determine the internal culture, the external values and the sentiment others hold about it.

My first company didn't serve me, I served it. I didn't allow it to pay me, give me days off or allow me to be sick. It didn't support my mental, physical and emotional health. I was at the bottom of the pile. As a result of this belief system, others abused my kindness, because I allowed them to. I believed the sole intent of my business was to serve others – from clients, to suppliers and stakeholders. I never built a salary in for myself. I thought I would pay myself once I could pay others. All seemed so honourable.

I existed to serve others

I was called a 'servant leader' by someone. I liked the term and it became my mantra. I existed to serve others. Of course, this was not sustainable. After 14 years of this attitude, the world crashed down around me.

My only saving grace was that my business did support my spiritual health, my soul. I knew it was doing good, that it was making a difference and it matched so many of my values of love, harmony, family – in the form of community. It did make me feel valued and full of purpose, and I guess this is how I kept going with the business for so long.

Let's focus on how to make sure you don't crash. Your business serves you first, so you can serve it and build the amazing business you have in your sights.

TECKS

You will be giving so much to your clients. The currency you have in life is your time, experience, commitment, knowledge and the skills to do good work for others. You need to feel worthy of money and you need to see the worth you have when you serve your clients.

I have created this formula to help clients work out how to charge for their time and also to give them a real sense of just how much they are passing on when they serve the needs of their clients.

Time + Experience + Commitment + Knowledge + Skills = £ value to others

(TECKS = £)

I am going to share a case study of a client who grew one of her clients to the point where they dominated so much of her time that she needed to increase their fees so she could hire someone to enable her to grow. This is a very common issue that can prevent growth.

We ran through these five questions together. I used the TECKS method to help her build her confidence and plan:

1. Time – how much time do you give to your client?

2. Experience – what experience are you bringing to them that solves problems for them?

3. Commitment – how committed are you to helping your client? Are you passionate about their success?

4. Knowledge – what is the knowledge you have accumulated that means you are the best person for them?

5. Skills – what are the skills you have to use your knowledge for, for their benefit?

How TECKS increased my client's fee by 40%

All clients want a great deal of justification to have their fees increased. This is how we used TECKS to show her client that she was worth more and was giving more value than they had originally expected. I will refer to my client as Jane.

Jane's story

Jane had been hired as a virtual assistant. She began with a number of clients providing back office roles such as bookkeeping, payroll, financial management, managing sales commissions and reporting on invoices raised. Over time she realised that she was taking on increased responsibilities. They crept in slowly, but clearly her client's confidence in her was growing, and he was asking her advice and including her in strategic decisions, involving her in recruitment and asking her to work on analysing numbers. The creep came in the form of extra calls, emails and connecting my client to an increasing number of people.

Jane was enjoying being helpful – kindness was one of her values in life. However, Jane approached me as she was starting to feel out of control and vulnerable to this one client, she was becoming more and more reliant on their fees as she was slowly closing down the business she had with her other clients. However, the amount she was charging her client was not compensating for this as they were still stuck in the original agreement.

This is a common issue for many small businesses. It is about capacity. When we work alone, we are limited by our own capacity. The joy of a client appreciating us is powerful as it makes us feel safe with them because they can't do without us. However, I know myself and from loads of clients I coach, clients can get rid of us very quickly when their needs change or they structure a business differently.

Jane agreed that it would be good to resubmit a proposal. In doing this, she would use the extra fees she would generate to bring another person into her business so she could keep growing her client base.

This is a copy of the TECKS report we did together that enabled Jane to negotiate and achieve a 40% increase in her fees, therefore enabling her to take on extra resources so she could grow. It is written in the first person as this is a copy of the exact report we wrote together and used to form the new proposal.

Jane's brainstorm on her new Client Proposal

Time

I am always on, always available, always thinking, regularly working through the night as my client works in different time zones. I am dedicated to the culture of XYZ company and the fast pace that decisions and solutions require. Very often the questions from their team come on demand, sometimes not always time managed, known and scheduled in advance.

Experience

I have run my own business and see the big picture in a business and its processes and needs. I have a diverse background within employment in the legal sector, plus four years of leading my company, which included building a business networking community that existed both online and offline.

Commitment

I was thrilled to win XYZ company as a client as it was my intention to continue to have a wider client base. However, I very quickly realised the demands of the client and how much I wanted to contribute and be a part of their growth. I wanted to add the value that a total commitment would enable. As a consequence, I reduced my commitment to growing other clients myself and spent more time with XYZ.

I am very committed to the success of others and to the growth of XYZ. I believe strongly in its mission and the culture that the owners believe in and are delivering.

I have my own entrepreneurial spirit and can relate very strongly to the sacrifices and commitment they have to their employees and company growth.

Knowledge

My knowledge is highly relevant to the requests that are being made of me. Business management and leadership, legal practices, financial management, customer service, team management and training, delegation, and the delivery of content and training. I understand the company culture well and feel part of the team already.

Skills

I have the ability to build teams and processes taking my knowledge and experience into consideration, while being able to roll my sleeves up and manage detail. I can also lead through delegation and sharing the vision that their board are so committed to and require their staff to buy into.

The win(s)

Incorporating this into Jane's proposal with the words she had written confirmed to her that the commitment and sacrifices she was making gave her the confidence to assert herself in her proposal to convince the client of her value. Jane achieved a 40% increase in her fees. This enabled Jane to build her own business further.

The increase in fees meant she could hire someone to manage the clients that she was no longer able to service directly and to grow the business further. In doing this, she regained control, reduced her vulnerability – the reality of it and the fear of it. She also reduced her workload through structure and began to think about some of her own personal needs.

Your time, experience, knowledge, commitment and skill are personal

We are in a period of commercial history when knowledge is being sold more than ever before. The majority of the people in my network are selling their knowledge and time for money by charging an hourly / daily fee or commanding a monthly retainer. Calling themselves consultants, coaches, speakers, mentors and advisors.

The ambiguity of when and how much to charge is very hard in a knowledge economy. Professionally qualified people such accountants, lawyers, architects and doctors charge a fee and no one ever challenges this. They may provide a free consultation (in some cases) and from then on you pay their fees. The personality traits of these professions ensures that they value their knowledge and they would never give it away.

Overdone strengths in financial negotiations

On the other hand, I have witnessed the brand building and online sharing of knowledge by millions of professional speakers, coaches, consultants and advisors over the past 20 years. They who have knowledge they want to sell and have built a diverse set of ways to deliver that knowledge. I know that sadly, many struggle to make ends meet despite their knowledge and experience. Many of these people are helpful, caring and love problem solving for others. They get a kick out of being helpful – it is a currency to them, so they often fail in seeing their financial value and often oversacrifice. An overdone strength that affects them as discussed in Chapter 6.

The variation in wealth in this knowledge sector is vast. From those who can fly around the world in personal jets through to those who struggle to pay for a train fare to meet a potential prospect.

What makes some people charge more than others?

Some of a person's financial success will be down to ambition, ego and the level of sacrifice they are willing to make. I don't believe it is just down to one person being more amazing than the other. I spoke earlier about success and ambition being personal to you. Some seek fame, adoration and massive wealth, almost celebrity status in their field. Others want to be a legend in a smaller way, satisfied with having an impact on fewer people, closer to home. All are undoubtedly driven to have impact and contribute and make the lives of those they serve better. It is your choice to create your own definition of ambition and measurement of success in your life. However, be aware of your overdone strengths and make sure your strengths stay in line with the ways to protect yourself from financial stress.

Your value is personal

A starting point in planning your pricing strategy is to know how much value you place on yourself and what you feel worthy of – your self-worth. A big lesson in life is that only you can place the value you feel that your time, experience, commitment, knowledge and skills have to others. What makes one person charge £100 and another £10 an hour? I have paid £600 for an hour of an expert's time and have paid a different expert only £60. I have been paid £500 for a speech and another time was paid £25,000.

We have to take into consideration market conditions, the reputation you have built, your brand and your ability to negotiate. It is also about what sector of the market you serve, ie the size of their wallet.

Selling products

I know that vast numbers of my readers will be selling their time. I am also aware that you may be selling products or a subscription model.

E-commerce has allowed many people to become product focused and sell products online. The internet has also allowed the delivery of a service to be sold as a subscription. Additionally, many people have used the internet to build a brand as an expert and sell their skills in passing on knowledge.

The time you spend on your company is still a calculation of TECKS and the worth you are to it. You should be able to build a business that serves you and gives you self-worth and esteem. Selling a product or a subscription is about setting up the processes in your business and managing the business model to ensure you get paid for your time. Efficiencies in your business and a great supply chain model will help you to ensure your time generates the value you seek.

Do TECKS on yourself by treating yourself as a client and see if there are areas you need to grow. Your time, your experience, your commitment, your knowledge and your skills. Are they all in line with the ambition you hold for your business?

In this chapter I want to focus more on the emotion of believing in yourself and using your time wisely. In the next chapter I talk more about the five basic skills you need.

Your impact is personal

Whatever we are selling, we have to sell the impact we will have on someone. From a dress or suit you bought to make you feel confident at an event, to the thousands you might spend on a coach to help you improve a particular part of your life and business, we are all seeking a shift from where we are to where we want to be.

Placing a value on your impact rather than on time is a great way to decide what you can and should charge. It should also be applied to products and services. Why am I willing to spend £500 on a suit jacket in one store but would not consider spending that on a weekend one? I personally place more value on what I look like in a business environment than I do when I am kicking around my home. It is personal to me how I value something. Equally, I would spend £50 for a back massage but would spend more on the skills and the impact of reflexology and reiki.

Of course, market conditions and the elasticity of price and economics comes into these decisions when setting price. I am not getting into that. I am more interested in how you value what you know and what you charge. In effect, this is the value you place on the impact you can have through the sharing of your time, experience, commitment, knowledge and skills, to deliver that impact.

What is the impact you have, and to whom?

I believe that when I spend time with a large company, I will impact them so much that they could increase their company's income by millions. I believe I can help an individual grow their business by thousands. The price I would charge a company would therefore be very different from what I would charge an individual. The ratio of impact would be the same, but the actual financial outcome would be different.

One of my clients has this model for charging. She states that her time with a large company could increase their income by £5m and as a result, she charges them 1% of that growth, invoicing £50,000.

For her smaller clients, who she loves to work with, she knows that her impact could help them grow by £50,000 for their first year, she charges them £500.

How you deliver these impacts has to be decided upon. For £50,000 she provides face to face time over a number of days. For £500 she provides a Zoom-based interview to learn about them and kick things off, followed by a month of WhatsApp mentoring and phone calls.

The critical point here is your impact. We are selling progress to our clients. If what we offer does not increase and improve the life, revenue, peace of mind or happiness of our clients then we are not able to value ourselves.

Finding the best model that suits you

Not everyone wants to provide one to one coaching and advice anymore. It can be exhausting and hard to scale. The growth in the expert who productises their knowledge and creates online courses is quite incredible. I hear about new experts, coaches, speakers and authors doing this every day. I have seen people create a volume product around their skills, producing these as online courses that once created, can make money while they sleep. Meanwhile they can sink their money into Facebook and Instagram advertising, having spent thousands on creating their online courses and sales funnels.

I have also seen the growth in e-commerce and the different ways someone might package and sell their products. Some go for high price and personal customer service, while others use the drop shipment and fulfilment method, never touching the product themselves but outsourcing the delivery. Then they promote through engaging and advertising on Instagram and Facebook, linking the advert through a back office system to their outsourced fulfilment centres.

The formula here is what works for you. So long as we are all ethical in our delivery and impact, knowing that if someone pays for a depersonalised online course, that they will still get the value from it they seek. Some experts are now out of reach for most of us as their time is of such value to them that we couldn't possibly afford them. They have priced themselves deliberately out of the common man's wallet. Instead, they have written books and online content. They have created events and can sell thousands of seats – after all, their fans and followers will always be eager for those rare moments to see them.

Your delivery method is personal to you

I beseech you not to get wrapped up in the trends that exist. Find the method of delivery that works for you. In this compare and despair world, I have watched the financial achievements of hundreds of people with their skills in building enormous global presence and selling online courses create a 'guru' brand and selling memberships. If this is something you seek, then there are many companies that can teach you this, courses you can sign up to and skills you can learn. First though, please make sure that what you are selling is desired and you have a reputation in your field to back it up. Also remember that technology has taken the heart and human element from interactions. So, never forget, we all want attention and to be treated as humans rather than a number.

Your price will determine the type of clients you get

I heard a brilliant lesson in pricing while hearing a talk from Lenka Lutonska, a sales coach. She shared a story from her past. She was starting out with her second business and desperate to make enough money to get by and feed her family. Her skills in mentoring, training and helping senior people in large companies were undisputed. She had many testimonials and a client referred her to a very senior board member of a company. Over the course of many conversations, she closed the deal and went on to provide a four-day, one to one course with this client.

After the four days, over a drink in the bar, he enthusiastically shared with her how it had been the best training he'd undertaken in his professional career. She asked him: "Why then were you so hesitant to buy from me?" These are key words for all of us to consider. He replied: "From what you quoted me, I would never have known the quality of training you provide. You were too cheap."

Finding the value in a market for your skills will take you time and will require taking some risks. Here is my story.

How I went from £1,000 to £25,000 in one conversation

I always charged around £1,000-£2,000 for my speaking engagements. One day, an event company called and asked if I could speak to the staff at one of their client's corporate days. The client was an airline company that wanted to help their cabin crew go part-time and grow their own businesses to supplement their income. My role was half a day in the cabin crew lounge giving one to one coaching. My initial thoughts were to charge £2,500. Then I took a look at my diary demands and my cash flow and decided I could risk not winning this particular client. I knew it was time to test my value as a speaker. And, as I didn't want to add any extra pressure to my already busy life, it had to be really worthwhile.

I moved the decimal point on my proposal and quoted £25,000. Nervously, I sent off the proposal and waited. Two days later the order arrived with a note stating: 'They were delighted to get someone of your calibre'. I took an educated risk, did not fear the loss and, in the end, I won. It is important for me to say that my integrity was intact as I believe the client also won. My motivation to impact the 50 or so people I spent time with was definitely greater, as was my confidence in myself and therefore my delivery and the outcomes for all.

Charging this price does not happen overnight. You have to build a reputation and also believe that you are worth it. I would never overcharge the value I can give. A great deal of this skill in quoting and negotiating comes from the emotion you hold about yourself. When your self-esteem is low, when you have taken many knocks or when you feel desperate, that is when it is hard to believe in yourself.

The epidemic of free

I am determined that you don't undervalue yourself so much that you give yourself away. When I shared my thoughts online about this subject, I created a huge discussion. Since the internet was born, we have seen many advantages to the business world and to humanity. We cannot ignore the many disadvantages too. One of them is the reduction in the value people place on knowledge. If I had a pound for every time someone has asked me for a one to one, to pick my brains, or get to know me, I would be a very rich person. Takers are takers and we must all beware.

Don't be a mug

Okay the tone of my voice is going to change now, as I have been so foolish in my own belief systems of life and I want to help you to avoid this. I have been a mug more times than I would like to remember. I get taken in by people and their need for help. I have made assumptions that someone cannot afford me and then I see the lifestyle they lead and the fact that they have perfected a way of treating people as mugs.

I have witnessed conversations from people like this who laugh in the face of the adversity of others and find it amusing. I hear: "Well if they are foolish enough to give their time away then let them, no wonder they are poor." It is a sad fact that some people are horrible.

Some people really lack integrity and they know how to play you. I have paid for coffees for people who have asked whether they can pick my brains, I have spoken for free at events when the owners of the events are fat cats and making a fortune out of my reputation and skills as a speaker. All of this is my overdone strength in life – I am too kind, too believing in other people's integrity.

It happens with large clients too. A friend of mine switched from being self-employed as a coach to working in the leadership development part of a large telecoms company. Her boss told her on day one of joining: "Enjoy this, you can get all sorts of amazing experts to come in and quote for business here. Pummel them for their knowledge and make them think you will order from them. Of course we won't, but it is a great way to get new, innovative thinking into our organisation."

The fact is that there are a lot of arse****s out there who are willing to treat you as a mug. Believe me and beware. Never give away your knowledge lightly. Be kind to those who genuinely need you, and qualify hard before you give your TECKS away.

Why has free become the new norm

The internet has connected us all and over time we have encouraged friendships online that have blurred the lines between business and friendship. The ease of access to people with skills, and the enormous desire for us all to be liked and to build a good reputation, has created a very confusing commercial world. Saying no to someone who is a relative stranger but knows you well online and asks you for coffee or a Skype call is hard to do. You cannot hide. Finding the right words to protect yourself from time wasters and people who seek to exploit your goodwill and knowledge is a hard thing to do.

This is when you have to remind yourself of the value of your time, the impact a coffee will have and to carefully qualify what motive the person has. This goes back to what I wrote about creating your boundaries, because this is potentially a breach of your boundaries. It is also about remaining in control, something I also discussed in that chapter. You have every right to ask what they would like to achieve in a meeting and place your boundaries of protection on it. This is business. Your time is your business. Being a friendly person in business does not mean becoming a poor person through your kindness.

One hour of your time and the creativity, inspiration and knowledge that you might pass on could have a radical impact on that person. They may go away energised, but the danger is that you leave feeling exhausted and drained. This is a time when you have to remind yourself that you are an asset to your business, and if you have just given away two hours of your time, then, once you know the hourly rate you cost your business, you will see the way you have allowed your business to be abused.

I am being deliberately black and white about this to make a point. Your whole self needs to be taken into consideration when you make these decisions. If you feel the meeting would reduce your loneliness, increase your reputation, give you a boost to your self-esteem and sense of worth, be useful in your research of a new service, then call it that. But ask yourself these questions before you say yes to a free meeting.

Being flexible is personal, but maintain your control

Once you have set a value on your service, there will be times when you deviate from this. For example, a client you want to work with, but who cannot afford your usual fee, makes an approach. It happens to be during a quiet time in your diary and you are willing to work for less to ensure some money comes in. You will know what feels right when you decide on a price reduction. This is about you being in control of your value and making a decision based on your choices.

Make sure your pricing is realistic and not the price you see others charge. The market will always dictate to a certain extent what it is willing to pay.

At times, I am willing to do a speech for free. I am also willing to have meetings for free on occasions. As long as I am in control and making the decision with the right reasoning behind it, I will never feel I have undervalued myself. You can never blame the other person if you are willing to reduce your price.

How I manage this is as follows:

1. I will do one speech a month for free, providing it is right for me. It either puts me in front of the right people or it suits my values of contribution.

2. I will discount my daily fees or speeches if I feel this person or company cannot pay me my usual fee and I want to help them, or I have more time than usual on my hands.

At all times, I will still produce an invoice. On that invoice I will show the discount I have given.

An invoice confirms this is a business decision and accounts for my time. Accounting for your time is very important in business. It shows you respect your business, whether it is just you in it, or you have a business partner, investors and staff.

How productive are you?

A great way to discipline yourself and ensure you are acting in the best interests of your business is to measure your productivity. Your business is reliant on you being very productive with your time and earning as much as possible for the business in the hours that you work.

An example would be:

- You generate £5,000 of income in a month
- You work 80 hours to do this
- Your hourly productivity is £5,000 divided by 80 = £62.50 per hour

When you record your time and fees, you will soon see whether the formula for your pricing and the processes behind your business are right. It is important that you include all the time you spend, not just the actual moment of delivering to a client. Every aspect of your business is about the revenue you generate.

In search of perfection

Creating value in a market starts with valuing ourselves. It also requires us to acknowledge and accept that we are not perfect. There is an underlying stress within many of us caused by seeking the perfect you. I see myself as someone who is in constant development, emotionally and intellectually. We are on a journey to find ourselves and to be in continual improvement.

The search for perfection, whether in our body image, emotional desires, money, or peace, whatever it is that occupies your mind can loop around your head, and it can be positive or negative. Good stress is powerful. Bad stress is dis-stress, much like dis-ease. We make ourselves uneasy and it can lead to the disease of the mind or the body.

In the next chapter I discuss the skills we need and the way we should approach constant development and aid our need for improvement. In business we must always apply ourselves to listening and learning, because this enables adaptation.

CHAPTER 11

Skills are Personal

"It Is not the strongest of the species that survives
but the most adaptable."

Charles Darwin

Learning to manage change and adapt to our environment is literally a survival technique, and this is true in business in these fast-moving times. We have a daily feed of the way disruption in business is impacting global economies. Our business, Ecademy, was ahead of the game, trailblazing the concept of social networking in business. Little did we know when we created it that even as an internet player, we would be disrupted by a new form of business model from LinkedIn, that of giving away a service for free.

Disruption, competition, global economic conditions, the ways government manage our lives, the way people vote, the mistakes, fake news and the integrity of people. And of course, the constant flow of new technology – now we hear of Blockchain, Crypto Currencies, and AI. All of these messages in our lives can impact not only our business but our motivation and dreams. Just when we think we have a business model and a marketing method that works well, we learn that the people or the platforms we rely on are changing. Facebook, is it popular anymore? Podcasting, does it work? Should I have a YouTube channel? Is Twitter effective? Should I now shift on to the Blockchain? Will I have to offer coins in order to trade?

Skills are personal

Keeping our skills in balance is important in order to manage the stress around this subject. In this chapter I want to discuss some of the fundamental skills we need. Skills are personal to you and I think there are some skills in business that can anchor us. Once we have these, we have a choice to make by deciding which skills are the 'must haves', which are 'nice to have', and which ones can be delegated to others.

I love the phrase 'when steering a boat, a captain can shift the wheel one degree and it drastically changes the course of the boat'. A small change through a growth in our skills can make an enormous difference.

In this chapter, applying the tools from the 'whole me' day planner, you may want to add some of the skills you feel you would benefit from gathering over the next year.

Your primary skills are your flame

In Chapter 7, I wrote about the aspects of your business that you love and that make you feel on fire and in your flow – your flame. These skills will be the ones that give you the confidence to go into business with a passion, a purpose, an acquired skill that you know you could sell, a product you know the market would love. You might be a bookkeeper, an artist, a writer, coder, marketer, a superb salesperson, a problem solver, a listener, a coach, a yoga instructor – the variety of skills my clients have is astounding. You know your deep skills, those things that you can trade in order to have a successful business.

Wrapped around your primary skill are all the secondary skills you have to acquire to manage your business. Some of these are mandatory and you have no choice but to acquire these skills. Once acquired, they are improved over time. Without them, your business and you will suffer.

Five fundamental skills you cannot ignore in business

1. Understanding business models – know what type of business life you want to have.

2. Knowing how to sell – your sales technique is personal.

3. Knowing how to build a brand that others can trust – your brand is personal.

4. Knowing how to manage finances – your finances are personal.

5. Knowing the digital technology that is critical to all businesses – digital is personal.

I am now going to run through each of these, sharing some of the things I have learned along the way.

1. Your business model is personal – first of the five fundamental skills you cannot ignore in business

You can choose the type of business life you want: stay self-employed as a solopreneur, create a scalable business, build a business for life, or create a business for exit. You can work from home, a co-working space, a coffee shop or be a digital nomad and live on beaches around the world. Deciding on the business model and lifestyle you want is a very important aspect of maintaining the control and the path of business that is right for you. If you don't make this decision, you will be like that pinball in the machine that throws you in all sorts of directions every time you read something someone else is doing.

Work anywhere any time – the new way

All around us we are seeing a change in mindset and working practices. I am constantly inspired by my adult children, aged 26, 24 and 21, by my nieces and nephews, 13 of them, and many of the young entrepreneurs I have mentored. The majority have chosen to work for themselves. Those who haven't are definitely 'intrepreneurs' within the companies they work for, seeking the same lifestyle and innovation in business that entrepreneurs seek. The interesting thing is that all of my nieces and nephews have had entrepreneurial parents but they have seen us apply a more rigid and traditional way of living and working.

In comparison to the Baby Boomer Generation, they work flexible hours, flexible days, in flexible places, doing flexible jobs and have many mini-breaks, not just the two weeks in the summer that we tend to afford and allow ourselves. Freedom is the most common word I hear when asking about their values.

What does freedom mean?

One of my mentees is a 31-year-old entrepreneur who told me that he has always been focused on achieving freedom in his life. I asked him if this was his number one value and without hesitation he replied "yes." When we dived further into this desire, it was clear that time was the commodity he was chasing. Time would give him the opportunity to achieve so much more in his life.

He shared with me the triangle of Time, Money and Energy. Drawing the triangle, he placed each word on the tips. He said that the issue we all have is that when we are students, we have time and energy but no money; when we are working adults we have money, energy but no time; and when we retire we have time, money but less energy.

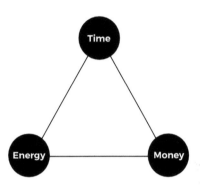

His focus and drive in life was to achieve freedom of time as soon as possible. Many people are now opting for the 'power of one', working alone and building a network of other solopreneurs to deliver their business services and products.

Unscaled not scale up

The book *Unscaled* by Hemant Taneja is a great read, sharing that the future of business is not about scaling up but rather about the drive towards agile business models with low costs, and flexibility. I quote a summary below of this book and see the sense in this theory. When you compare this with the business models of the past that were built around control, ownership, employment and fixed offices and costs, you can see the attraction to this model in the Millennial Generation and to the enlightened among us oldies!

"Throughout the twentieth century, technology and economics drove a dominant logic: bigger was almost always better. It was smart to scale up – to take advantage of classic economies of scale. But in the unscaled economy, size and scale have become a liability. Today's most successful companies – Uber, Airbnb, Amazon, Salesforce – have defied the traditional 'economies of scale' approach by renting scale instead of spending vast amounts of money building it. And a new generation of upstarts is using artificial intelligence to automate tasks that once required expensive investment, enabling them to grow big without the bloat of giant organisations."

Clearly the digital world enables this new lifestyle. Let me share a story that inspires me.

Being a POWERnomad

Consider the triangle of time, money and energy I shared. The working adult was seen to have money and energy but no time; with a different attitude and business model we could gain more time to nurture and ensure our whole self stays well.

The term nomad is a lifestyle choice to live nomadically. My daughter, Hannah, left employment in a fabulous company that had taken her in as a graduate and gave her amazing skills. Like many of the graduates she joined with, she eventually wanted to start her own business. Having lived well with a good salary, she didn't want to do what many people do when they start a business, she did not want to live in scarcity. She was used to a certain standard of living and lifestyle.

Hannah moved to Bali to live a life that would enable her to still live well. By doing this, she eliminated the stress of scarcity that many startups I know have in order to build a business. This enabled cash reserves to be built, enabled her to delegate her wax so she could focus on her flame, her strengths. She networked within the Facebook groups that hold so many global digital nomads and built a team of other highly skilled people. She built her company POWERnomads.

I love this for so many reasons. The main one being exactly the purpose of this book – Hannah started her business looking after her whole self with all the wellbeing habits built in from the start: massages, yoga, rest, good food and exercise. In other words, she looked after her emotions, mind, soul and body.

Business is personal and what is more important than to choose the way you want to live your life while you build and thrive within it?

How we are all migrating to this mindset

Each day when I wake, if I am working from home, I consider the work I have to achieve and consider the type of environment I want to be in. I never feel I have to work at a desk. I think of the vibe I need and I go and find the right place.

Not all of us can fly away to a beautiful island. However, we can cut ourselves some slack when it comes to the rules and the disciplines many of us learned when employed, and enjoy a fuller life. Discipline and focused work is important. What I advocate here is that we do it in a way that works for us, in places that work for us. Finding your business model is about finding the mindset and the skills for business that work best for you.

2. Selling is personal – second of the five fundamental skills you cannot ignore in business

None of us have a business if we fear or avoid the sales process. I know large numbers of people who think they are selling when they are chatting online and attending the same networking events. I don't deny that these conversations can lead to business, but we have to be careful not to hide behind the social aspect of business networking and forgetting that we do need to sell.

If the statement above makes you take a breath, then there is a danger that this is how you are. I know I tend to rely on the reputation I am building all the time and the 'chat'. Selling is a pain for many small businesses: we are selling ourselves, creating the processes and forcing ourselves to create a way for people to give us their order.

We have to do some things even if we don't like them

I was recently with Mike Southon, author of *The Beermat Entrepreneur* and *Sales on a Beermat*. He is one of the most prolific sales people I know and has been a role model to me regarding the tenacity, flexibility and creativity of selling throughout his life. Over lunch he told me that he has never stopped having nervous energy around a sale. He believes this is something we have to drive on through, and accept.

I thought about this and remembered my best friend telling me how she hated the thought of exercise, and yet for the past 30 years I had held her up as my exercise guru, my fittest friend – and I assumed she loved it.

I heard a radio interview with the phenomenal singer and composer Ed Sheeran where he said that he "loved playing the guitar and singing" but he disliked interviews. He just accepted that this was all part of being able to live the life he wanted.

Selling is something we just have to accept and get on with, and it can be fun.

Selling is still selling – digital technology can't change everything

I grew up in business through the 1980s and 1990s, managing 300 telesales and field staff in the IT sector. I was taught the process of suspects, prospects, customers. This seems such an old-fashioned set of words. Now we now have 'followers' and we 'network'. We build our brand. Too many of the clients I have coached hope that by some amazing serendipity, customers will come to them.

The funnel of selling has been extended with social media. It starts with people getting to know you exist, people then 'liking' content, then choosing to 'follow' you more closely. However, at some point you must have a process to see them as a potential client (suspect), find a way to qualify them (prospect) and then close them into a customer.

Having a vision for your business is the starting point

Jack Daly, author of *Hyper Sales Growth*, shared an amazing and quite life-changing moment for me on stage at an event I was also speaking at on the Gold Coast of Australia. I was mesmerised by this man. His energy and his commitment to us all being sales people at heart, no matter what our core business skills were. Jack shared with us the fundamentals of having a vision and how this isn't a mission statement, but rather "it is far 'grander' than that," Jack says, "it is the spark of excitement that makes someone take a risk, the dream you sell the client. They have to see the future you are offering them, feel it, want it and commit to it."

These words from *The Little Prince* say it beautifully.

"If you want to build a ship, don't drum up the people to gather wood, divide the work, and give orders. Instead, teach them to yearn for the vast and endless sea."

Antoine de Saint-Exupéry

You have to put on your sales face

In Chapter 10 on The Value You Place on Yourself is Personal, I wrote about the need to value what you bring to the client. The confidence in your TECKS, the time you will give your client, the experience you bring, the commitment to their problem, the knowledge you share, and the skills you have acquired, will all help with your confidence.

At some point though, you do need to put on your sales face and start selling. Success will be the best way to raise your confidence and confirm the worth you have to others. You will not know it until you try, try and try again.

You cannot fear rejection

We all get rejected and like the actor who constantly attends auditions, if you want it enough, you will try, try, try again. My son Ross is a gifted actor and he held lead parts throughout school. When he was trying to get into acting school, he asked me: "When will I know if I want this enough?" and I said "When you give up." It gave him a jolt, it felt almost cruel of me. However, I was right and when he did give up, he just said: "Mum, I didn't want it enough."

Where are your clients?

Selling is more complicated now, we have such a global reach and we may know many people who mostly fall into the 'advocate' bucket. Your 'social capital' are the people who believe you are an amazing resource but will not necessarily be your customer. They might talk about you in the market, give you a great reputation and increase your credibility through their validation of you, but they are not part of your prospect list. Social media has created a distraction as well as an opportunity. The self-awareness you need to keep when you are using social media and how it is really serving you and your business is very important.

In this section I want to remove you from the modern world for a few minutes... not for long.

How I learned to sell

In 1985 I was taught an invaluable formula by Mercuri International.

The QQD Formula – quantity, quality and direction

The reason I love this process so much is that it gives me control of my sales campaign, and I can measure the outcomes and fine-tune my weaknesses as they show up.

QQD works on the principle of making the right:

- Quantity – of calls/contacts
- Quality – the skills to deliver your pitch against the opportunity
- Direction – ensuring you have pre-qualified and know this type of prospect has the need

Quantity + Quality + Direction = a closed sale

Once you have calculated the quantity of sales you need in order to achieve your financial target, you then make sure that the quality of your proposition is awesome, then you ensure that you direct all of your effort at the person who is most likely to need your product or service.

Quantity

You need to know the revenue target required and the quantity of business you need. I have had this discussion with so many startups and small businesses and even in large companies; while this seems quite basic it can be easy to forget the basic things in selling.

Being in control of your life means knowing what you have to do to achieve the success you are striving for. It is hard to be in control without all the facts at your disposal. The quantity of clients you need is part of being in control. Ask yourself these very fundamental questions regularly – it forms part of your business plan.

Example of a quick quantity test

Create a spreadsheet that has a list of your services and / or products, in the next column place the gross profit you make in them (at this stage don't worry about the costs of running your business, this is your net profit). Then mark against each item how many customers you can sell to each month on average. The final column is the total net profit you make on each item. At the bottom of that column you will see the total profit you can generate.

Here is an example – don't worry too much about how I have priced them, they are examples and not suggestions of your value.

Product/service	Total gross profit	Monthly customers required	Total income
Consulting fees	3,500	1	3,500
Speaking fees	500	2	1,000
Coaching – face to face	300	2	600
Coaching – Skype clients	150	6	900
Workshop to 10 people	300	10	3,000
Advertising on Podcast channel	30	5	150
		27	9,150

This is a LIVE example of a client of mine. He was selling time, so he had no production costs. We calculated this based on gross profit, excluding VAT. Generating this helped him see that each month he needed to find and service 27 clients to achieve the gross profit of £9,150 a month. Of course, his costs and taxes brought down the actual money he could have as family income. But the point here is that we need to see the total number of customers we must generate in order to focus selling online, and not just make a noise online.

Quality

Let's take this client example into the next phase. We needed to ensure he had the best chance of converting the people he was having conversations with. We needed to ensure the quality of his selling, sales pitch and the ability to match his closing words to the needs of the potential customer was in place. Identifying your areas for development around this part of the process is important. It is too individual and lengthy to include in this book, but my goal is to alert you to the emotions you might have of frustration, disappointment or even fear, and to encourage you to get these skills from a great sales coach.

You are in control of the quality of your work, and it is your choice as to whether to put your energy into improving this.

There is too much competition in the market for the attention you seek from your 'suspect' to hope for sales. Those who win a client are not necessarily cleverer or harder working, they might be applying more effort to this aspect of the sales process.

Social media can kill the skills to sell

Too many of the small business people I speak to rely on social media as a funnel to close business. I believe that social media, the dangers of automation and shallow communication online is what has created a low level of sales skills. I have experienced many LinkedIn requests to connect from people seeking to sell to me. However, their attention and respect for this part of the process is so slap-dash. They rarely show any evidence that they have read my profile, let alone made an effort to customise the first connection with me to illustrate they are genuinely interested in me. This part of selling is about identifying your prospects, showing an interest, asking questions and finding a way to have a conversation.

Bad selling because of the hands-off, automated world

Last year, I decided I wanted to spend considerable money on my social media channels and website. I wanted to buy from someone local to me and asked around within my networking group to see who they would recommend. Anyone who Googles me will see I have a good number of connections across the social channels and therefore am not a beginner. They could also discover with just a little bit of Googling that I was awarded my OBE by the Queen in 2014 for my Contribution to the Social Digital Sector. I was not a muppet as my husband would call it.

Someone connected me to a friend of theirs and so I emailed back and asked for a phone call with the potential supplier.

Ready to get my credit card out and solve a problem that had been niggling me, I looked forward to the call. The reply I got less than 10 minutes after my email was a templated, copy and pasted reply, stating how excited she was to help me begin my social journey and that she loved working with beginners.

Needless to say, I did not reply. The sale was dead. A beautiful lead, literally handed to her on a plate, but absolutely no quality of selling applied to the process of qualifying and closing the sale. We have to remember that all potential clients have a desire to be interesting and wanted. The more you can make them feel special and understood, the higher your chances of success.

Volume minds kill individual sales

The danger is that many people are thinking volume now, adding automated processes to save time and failing to connect on a deeper level, failing to ask questions, failing to listen and ultimately, failing to show they care. We want our clients to go into our sales funnel. We need to calm down, consider the sale and most importantly, consider the potential customer.

Make it easy for someone to buy from you

By now you know I don't want everyone to default to automation and processes in selling. We all know how annoying it is when the phone companies and banks force us down their processes. We feel unwanted. I suggest you look at your sales process and make it as easy as possible to let a prospect buy from you.

Automation can be great. One of the best examples of this is the 1-click that Amazon has implemented. I believe that their dominance is due to the ease of buying. However, it is a balance we need to find by never overstretching the automation to the frustration of the potential client. Gaining the attention of anyone takes a huge amount of work and investment, and I hate it when someone loses a client because they stumbled at the last hurdle, the place when a conversation on the phone or face to face would have nailed it.

The blend of human interaction and automation is essential. Your user journey from suspect to customer might be the one aspect of all your work that is failing you.

Direction of effort and language

I know that many startups and small businesses want to keep the net as wide as possible in order to maximise their opportunity to gain a client. The reality is though, when we speak the language of the perfect client, we succeed in attracting them. No different from the different types of bait a fisherman uses to attract the type of fish he wants.

The way you direct your effort is the final part of the QQD formula. There are two aspects of this that I will discuss now:

- Where can your perfect clients can be found?
- What type of personality do they have?

Where is your perfect client?

I love using Twitter, Instagram and Facebook. This is where my tribe hangs out, the people I relate to, feel good around and where I can be me. However, as I mentioned earlier, we need to find where my potential clients hang out.

Once we have decided the most likely place to fish, we need to direct our effort and build credibility and connections in that social pond. This is actually so obvious that I am not going to spend too much time with you on this subject now, but you should spend time thinking about it and researching this. Wherever they are, get to know that place, whether online or offline. Find the networking groups, the events, the conferences. Become part of their world.

If you can find them online, start by noticing their content. Don't just 'like' it, share it and comment on it and start the conversation.

What is the character and personality of your perfect client?

There are a number of psychological and analytical tools in the market that help us to understand our personality traits and communication styles. These different tools form the general conclusion that there are four personality types. Carl Jung divided personalities into two main groups, introverts and extroverts, and then into four subtypes that were about the way these people see the world.

For over 10 years, I have used a tool for my business called iMA. It stands for Identify, Modify and Adapt and was developed by James Knight. Within this tool you can learn your communication style. I want to apply it to how we should treat the four different types of client you might be talking to.

How iMA helped me

Sales coach Alison Edgar, author of *Secrets of Successful Sales*, also uses iMA. She uses iMA to help her clients understand their personal limitations and overcome the fear of selling. Discussing my sales traits with her, it is clear that my personality is very passionate and emotionally driven. I like to help others and see most things from the angle of why and purpose. Naturally, when I am selling, I want to engage the client, get them to like me, talk about the passion I hold for what I am selling and very often focus my pitch on the social impact my product will have.

This all sounds great. However, this form of selling does not work for everyone I meet as there are four main personality traits which iMA identifies as: High Blues, High Yellows, High Reds and High Greens.

Adapting my sales technique has been a steep learning curve for me. I have to honour the fact that not all people communicate in the same way as I do or have the same values.

What is your natural communication style?

I want to list the four types of iMA styles that people have as this is a key component in the way you direct your sales proposition.

Remember, iMA stands for Identify, Modify and Adapt. When you identify your client's personality, modify and adapt the way you direct your pitch, and you will achieve a greater conversion rate.

If you haven't done this yet, go to http://ima-power.com. It is free to do and will take you less than five minutes to complete. Each of the four personality styles are called High because they are the dominant style. Of course, we all have a bit of everything as we adapt to different situations, but here I am listing the ways in which you should sell to each colour. When reading them all, consider the irritation when we sell to them with the wrong tone and communication style.

iMA High Blue

Summary of style – non-assertive, open and people-oriented

This style bases their communication style on depth. They like to form relationships and are non-assertive. They like conversation and to get to know the person selling to them.

When selling to them, they want you to be pleasant and gentle, non-assertive, consistent, selfless, open, sincere and supportive of their feelings, as well as interested in their lives, especially why they do what they do. Your High Blue client will want to know how your solution will help and support them.

iMA High Yellow

Summary of style – assertive, open and people-oriented

The High Yellow is an assertive character (remember assertive does not mean aggressive). You know where you are with this type of person. They will be positive and friendly, but they like to get things done quickly. They like you to show flexibility, so they feel that they are in control, they are impatient, so deliver your message quite quickly, let them do a lot of the talking, show positivity and excitement. You should be open with your message to gain their trust and generous with your praise. Showing a great deal of support and listening to their ideas will flatter them.

The High Yellow wants to be at the forefront as they are creative, so show how innovative you are with your approach. They also want to collaborate and feel that their ideas have value and are important. You must not be a 'know it all' with this person as they love to be recognised as leaders in their own way. They also like to have fun and will love it if you know lots of people they think they should also know as they are connectors on steroids!

iMA High Red

Summary of style – assertive, closed and task-oriented

The High Reds want a return on investment. They look for practical solutions and feel time starved. The High Reds are great at delegating and won't want to get bogged down with detail until they show a level of interest. When that happens they will feel safe in their decision. They have no time for people. The task is what they focus on rather than being relationship focused because they want to get things done. They don't want lengthy conversations, and they want you to respect their time.

To sell to this personality type you need to be very organised, thoroughly researched on their company and them. They tend to have higher egos. Always stay practical, brief, respectfully assertive, fast and to the point. You will not get a long meeting with them, so many High Reds I support mark about 30 minutes in their diary, sometimes we overrun, providing they want to, but they want to be in control of their time. They are 'what people'. What can be achieved? What will you do? What do we need to do? You must always demonstrate how your solution will help them achieve their personal success.

iMA High Green

Summary of style – non-assertive, closed and task-oriented

High Greens are analytical, they want to understand what can be achieved. They take a logical approach and are focused, just like the High Reds, on the task more than the people. They are non-assertive and like the High Blues, need you to be supportive, but rather than of their feelings (as in the High Blues), they want you to support their thoughts. If you want to sell to this type of person you must be time disciplined, very logical and precise. They love facts, statistics and evidence. You must display your knowledge well and be researched and prepared. They like structure and rules. The High Green takes absolute pride in doing a great job, so demonstrate to them in great detail how your solution will help them achieve the objectives they have, which are to add value through knowledge and information.

How to assess quickly what colour your client is

It is not always possible to get clients to take an iMA test before you meet them (although I have achieved this on a number of occasions). Most of the time you need to assess them yourself and fast.

When you meet them, quickly work out how they are making you feel. If you feel comfortable and at ease, they are likely to be High Yellows or High Blues. These are people-focused. If they make you feel you need to work really hard to gain their trust, and they say little to you when you talk, they are likely to be High Reds or Greens, very focused on the task. Assessing whether the person in front of you is people- or task-focused, assertive or unassertive becomes easier the more you apply this. Have some fun with your own family and friends – try to guess what they are and then ask them to take the test. The more you get involved with this tool, the more you will be able to identify someone by their behaviour.

Your sales process is personal to you and to others

How you sell, who you sell to and what you sell is personal and making sure that you structure your sales life to suit you is very important.

I know that many people prefer a hands-off approach to selling, and while I respect that, I personally like to engage and know people, probably because I am a High Blue. What is important in this section is that you identify what works for you and what skills you need in order to achieve your version of success.

We all get wrapped up in our passions and what we need to achieve. This can sometimes impact the outcome we want. When selling, we must remember that we are seeking to solve our client's problem, not our own.

When I applied a QQD formula to my sales process and incorporated the iMA tool, my conversion rate was high. If you consider my earlier client in the Quantity section, he needed to have 27 clients each month. The better skilled you are, and the more you direct your effort and communication in the right way, the better your conversion rate will be.

3. Your brand is personal – build a brand that others trust is the third of the five fundamental skills you cannot ignore in business

I think the greatest asset we can build throughout our lives is trust. We all seek to trust one another and know that the integrity of the people we do business with is solid and they will not let us down.

The online world provides many opportunities for your trusted connections to say good things about you, to build your credibility and to validate who you are. It is not enough to have a massive following. The sad fact is, technology can be gamed. The written words in testimonials and the real sharing of ourselves speaks volumes in gaining trust. Your online brand is critical for validation of your business. You need to be found and you need the potential client, partner, investor or supplier to read good things and see the relevance of your work.

In 2009 I wrote *Know Me, Like Me, Follow Me*. In this book, I shared how to build your online brand and become known, liked and followed. I am not going to write a guide to social media in this section as I could easily go off-piste from the purpose of this book. What I want to share here is that social media can be incredibly damaging to a business if used in the wrong way.

Social media is broadcast. Podcasting, blogging, YouTube – these are all ways to achieve your brand, a one-to-many approach to promote your company.

Building brand one person at a time

Twitter, LinkedIn and Facebook are the social networking aspects of the new world in communication. I believe, while they can be one-to-many, the real joy and potential of these are the opportunity to have conversations and get to know others, to show we are interested, advocate for them, build a true connection and find those who share our same interests. Too many people still use it to broadcast, forgetting that it is all very well to build a brand and be known, but being liked is also important.

The other danger of building automation into a business is that you may miss the channels your potential client might like most in order to talk to you. Everyone has a preferred communication channel. The choice of how to communicate with people now is vast: WhatsApp, SME, email, iMessenger, Twitter Direct Message, and LinkedIn Private Messaging. We now have to be open to all channels and know which one our clients most prefer. We cannot force our clients into our favourite channels.

Brand building is not about ego

Four years ago, I was invited to a CBI Annual Dinner, a posh event. I discovered that I was on a table with some very successful corporate leaders and I was the only entrepreneur. When I sat down for dinner, the gentleman to my right introduced himself as being from a large telecoms brand and then said to me: "I know you are Penny Power, I Googled your name and was shocked to find how much you like having your name blazed around the place."

This is how I replied: "Imagine you went into your company tomorrow to find your car parking space had gone. You finally park your car and walk in. A security guy stops you and advises you that you have been fired and your pass no longer works. Tell me, Andrew," I said, "how will you make a living from that day onwards? Who are you? What are your skills? How would your potential clients know you are any good?"

He shuddered, smiled and said: touché. We laughed and then he spent the next three hours asking me how to build his online brand.

When you are selling your skills to others, there is no greater relief for the potential client than if they can Google you and you appear at the top with lots of content that proves your knowledge and also speaks to them with empathy.

Be you online

So many people try to build a corporate brand despite being a small business. They also fear sharing their story, the very story that illustrates that your knowledge is not purely academic, that it comes from true passion and understanding as your own personal journey has been like theirs.

You are not a corporate cog in a wheel of vastness. You are a determined individual who wants to help others with their journey. You should not try to be anyone else. Your brand is YOU. People are buying you. They are not buying the large brand or the Amazon machine. They are buying the lovely person who wants to have an impact, and you are the reason they want you to be their supplier.

Don't hide yourself, but be proud and confident in yourself. Your source of happiness and success sits in the real you that others want to know.

4. Finance is personal – knowing how to manage finance is the fourth of the five fundamental skills you cannot ignore in business

Earlier in the book, I shared the importance of knowing 'what' your monster is in your business stress. For many it is the flow of money. The worry of a dry bank account and the fear as they look into the distance that they will not have the cash their business needs. This emotion of fear can change when you achieve a relationship with money. When you make friends with the money monster you no longer fear it.

It is hard to control money, but you can let go of fear

Security in any relationship comes with understanding. A girlfriend who wants to see her boyfriend every night, but he wants to go out with the lads, might feel insecure. She seeks control, wants to dominate and can never find peace. The day she reconciles with herself and realises that she needs to let go of her fears, and realise that the boyfriend is not disloyal or out to hurt her, is the day she finds peace.

Money is like this. It has the power to dominate us. When we have it, we feel good; when we don't, we feel out of control and we feel bad.

To be in business we must understand money. We must learn to love finance, we must learn to enjoy managing our cash flow and learn to honour our admin days when we are chasing money or sending invoices. Money is an energy. It can be a good one or a bad one. It can be your friend or your enemy. One thing is for certain, if you don't build a relationship with it through the good and the bad, you will never be able to cope with being in business.

Gaining skills in cash flow is not hard – ask a friend

A digital marketing consultant I have known and admired for over 15 years, a friend online, shared her story of learning how money works. Nicola Cairncross now lives in Greece, having lived in England her whole life. Her life as a child was one of scarcity. Her mother worked hard to build a business and all resources went into the business, which meant her childhood was challenging financially. Her goal in life was to build her own business and create financial freedom.

Nicola did not lack the skills to sell, serve clients, create and work hard. However, in the early days she came unstuck purely due to the management of money within the business. She asked her bank manager to help her with this and he advised her to ask an accountant, saying he didn't know either. The accountancy people she asked just said they would do her accounts and tax returns, 'it was not their job to train her'. It was a friend who came to her rescue and taught her how to do a weekly cash flow, how to see the flow of the money from clients, booked and not paid for business, and how to leverage credit without getting into debt.

My experience of this whole subject, from speaking to people and from the hard knocks of life, is that very few people know this skill. Even CEOs of businesses who have delegated all their lives don't have it. I know this from the clients I have helped.

Don't hesitate to ask for help. Find someone to show you this business skill. Don't be embarrassed, we all need to learn it.

Your moral code and money

Two things in business happen with money: income and outgoings. It is that simple. The challenge comes when you have more outgoings than income. This is where you risk being insolvent, which is illegal. To owe more money than you are owed is a dangerous position to be in as, in effect, you are stealing. If you take on a supplier, and you know you will not be able to pay them, then you are using a moral code in business that defines your attitude and your values.

We live in an ecosystem together, we co-exist

I believe as entrepreneurs, especially the solopreneurs among us, that we live in an ecosystem together. The balance and energy of that system relies on mutual respect, and when one of the members of that ecosystem disrupts the energy and balance of it by having low moral codes, we are all impacted. It is our duty to put good energy into this community. We must all rise together, or we might all fall together.

I have seen amazing business owners, for example single hard-working mums, who become destroyed by clients who don't pay them. I make it my business to know who these non-payers are, and I avoid them like the plague. The communication we all have with one another as solopreneurs and small business owners is random and open, and when one person fails to pay, you can bet hundreds of us will get to hear about this. The impact of debt on a small business is both personal and damaging. I cannot tolerate any person or brand who holds back payment, delays or fails to pay.

Manage your contracts

Stress in business comes when we have not invested the time to set up the processes that protect us. It also happens when we have an expectation of others that they follow our own moral code, and rarely is that the case.

Understanding your cash flow is an absolute minimal need for any business. The reason I cover this here is because of the consequences to your emotional and mental wellbeing when this skill is not learned. It should be given the due respect it deserves.

5. Digital technology – the last of the five fundamental skills you cannot ignore in business

Earlier I wrote about your primary skills, the skills that gave you the courage to start a business and the knowledge of how you give value to others, while earning revenue and profiting from it.

Much of any business's profit is held within the efficiencies it has. You have a limited amount of time and the more you can apply that time to finding customers and closing the sale, the more profit you will make.

Digital applications that aid with your finance and back office processes – the social online channels such as Facebook, Twitter, Instagram and LinkedIn, the marketplaces such as Amazon, Shopify and eBay – are incredibly powerful. Whether managing your money, delivering your service, or selling your products, digital solutions will make life more efficient and create a more productive business.

The carpet fitter

Knowing what to use that has the most impact in the fastest possible time is all about awareness of your business and where the challenges and needs lie. Our priorities around digital applications are personal to our business needs. Let me share a story that highlights this.

Four years ago, I had a client who was in deep stress. He had been a carpet fitter for 20 years and was contracted to a number of carpet shops. One day he and his sister decided to open their own carpet shop. They took on the costs of rent, staff and stock and soon realised that with all their money sunk into the business, they hadn't been able to pay themselves for four months, despite working harder than ever. He was crying while he shared this with me – a large, muscled, tattooed man was crying from the stress this put him under.

I asked him where the most stressful aspect lay. He replied that it was the warehouse costs for all the remnants he was storing. He said most of the profit lay in the parts of the carpets that were left over after fitting them.

I asked him whether he realised how many people bought carpet remnants on eBay. He had no idea this was the case and within five days of our conversation, he had his remnants on eBay and was hearing the ting of online sales. When I next met him, he was a changed man. Having learned the power of this digital skill, he went on to look at all his processes and little by little, he was going digital.

The new mum – the new solopreneur

One of my mentees was a new mum. She had left employment and become a reiki practitioner and reflexologist. She made this life-changing decision to give her more time with her baby, but her bookkeeping was getting her down. Finding the time each week meant she and her husband rarely had time together at the weekends. She discovered a great solution online for her receipts and bookkeeping. As a result, she found she could complete all her admin in the gaps in her day, often while sitting on people's drives waiting for her appointment slot. She gained her weekends back.

Never exploit the expert when gaining skills

In Chapter 10 The Value You Place on Yourself Is Personal, I write about the epidemic of free. Free is the expectation that you should give away your time and knowledge for free.

I am very sensitive to those who have dedicated time to learn a craft, to learn a digital application, to study. They have invested time and effort, and have a unique knowledge that can be easily exploited. I don't want you to do that to others.

You have to find your own moral code around how you gain knowledge. One thing I ask of all small businesses and startups is that they don't exploit a fellow small business. The epidemic of 'may I pick your brain', or 'can I have a one to one to ask you for help' is impacting all small businesses. While it may be a good way to expand your knowledge and network, it is parasitic. I would always offer a small token of money to anyone who has a secondary skill that would save me hours of time to learn myself. I care so deeply about this that I am working on a solution to help the transfer of skills, called 'Skills Orchard'.

If you want to learn how to use a digital application, consider that the person who may be willing to show it to you will have invested hours and hours learning this themselves. It took my business partner Gail Thomas 26 hours to fully learn the Facebook Advertising Engine. She says she would have been happy to pay someone who has also gone through it in order to show her what they know, saving her 25 hours of time, thus increasing her productivity ratio.

You do not have a business if you cannot pay suppliers

All businesses need to have costs built into their business. Too many people I meet say that they can't have costs. If that is the case, I fear you have to take a lot from others in order to build a business. Consider your moral code and your own values around this. It doesn't take long for a network to learn this pattern and they will soon lock out and avoid those who do this.

I have enjoyed sharing my journey with you, and the mix of amazing attributes and skills you have. My focus has been on ensuring that you honour the amazing person you are, and acknowledge the courage and determination you show each day. The final chapter is a wrap-up, a way to give you the boost you need to be yourself, knowing that you are amazing.

CHAPTER 12

Your Future is Personal

Taking positive action in the new world – become the person you know you are

Throughout our journey together, I have visualised you and written to you as a friend. I have shared some of my dark moments and many of my lessons in life, and how I turned my thinking and thoughts of success and happiness around.

In this chapter I want you to find your voice, make the right choices for you and take positive action in this connected economy.

My research over the years, taken from the large number of deep conversations I've had, and through leading communities, is that when we dig deep into anyone's life, no one is content with every aspect of their lives. Accepting this fact can, in itself, release fear and enable a brighter life. The compare and despair world we find ourselves in has caused a great deal of anxiety in many of us. Even thinking about anxiety gives us anxiety because thinking we are low can make us feel even lower. We overthink, and we strive for a perfect life.

When the internet launched and became a vast intrusion, and perhaps opportunity, in our lives, we were not able to go back to our childhood and learn how to be part of this. We have all adapted in real time. The internet has impacted our businesses and our personal lives. It has caused a cultural change in communication and here we all stand, part of it, whether we wanted it or not.

I believe that the connected world is a force for good, yet we are all part of the transition from an unconnected world to a connected one. We cannot expect a revolutionary shift in the global economies to be easy or painless. The saying I have heard most this year is: 'it is what it is'. I don't believe this is a phrase stated in a negative, disempowered way. No, I believe it is about acceptance.

Acceptance

For me, one of the most powerful tools I have used in my life is acceptance. This is not the same as surrendering, but rather it is about saying 'some things I cannot change'. You cannot change your past, yet your past can limit you if you don't just accept it. We also need to appreciate that we may hold expectations of others that are not met. We may also hold expectations of certain aspects of our lives that, again, have not been met.

I learned that if I had truly understood my values through the first 54 years of my life, then my own definition of success, of ambition and happiness, was actually the life I had succeeded in creating. It seems that my values led me more than my daily intent for a different definition of success.

Unrequited success

I am aware that there are many of us who are frustrated and disappointed with our success. Like the feeling of unrequited love, we feel that we have put so much of ourselves into the relationship between our business and ourselves. We love our business and hold a deep relationship with it, and we hope that it will return us the energy of success, happiness and financial peace that matches all that we gave it. We have defined who we are by what we are. Getting back in touch with the power of our 'who' can make all the difference to our future peace of mind.

Childhood and early adulthood experiences do impact us as they frame our beliefs and our thoughts, which can invisibly influence our lives more than we are aware of.

Unrequited success is all around us: from the businessman who has been challenged by the new business world, to the businesswoman who developed her career during a powerful period in the world when the Prime Minister of the UK was a woman, when many women around the world were being supported and empowered to succeed by their peers and the media. In a world when women were told they were equal, but the culture around them in some businesses and organisations did not reflect that, both men and women find themselves in a world of transition. Leading the change and not fearing it, allowing and accepting that we are all the torchbearers of this change for ourselves and for the next generation, will help us all thrive into the future.

Stop being limited by your past

"Your battle scars are the most powerful gifts you have been given. Use them to move forward, not hold yourself back."

Penny Power OBE

I have learned that I am successful, I am happy, I am loved, and I am worthy. I focus on what my values are and reflect on my life with that filter. The adversity in my life has made me the person I am. I have sometimes loved more deeply than the love I received. I empathise more deeply due to the lack of kindness I have received. I built community because I knew what loneliness was like. I am what I am because of, not despite these things.

My sharing in this book has been deliberately open, and it is given to you with the amount of love I wish I had received when I was learning to build a business. We need love and we need to love ourselves. When we love ourselves, it means we accept all aspects of who we are, and from that comes the understanding that we have become worthy of our success. The feeling of love means that we trust and don't fear. When we are in this state of mind, life flows far better.

In the closing words of this book, I want you to seek out the values that give you joy and fulfilment. I want you to understand, embrace and work with your personal emotional traits, to find ways to accept that so many aspects of your negative inner voice are the same as other people's — because they are human. Try to remove the beliefs that you have lived by that have held you back and have the confidence to stand as tall as the person you are inside. Strive to find new empowering beliefs and make them powerful for you and for others.

We are who we are, and sometimes 'it is what it is'. Acceptance, managing our minds and learning to live the life in the values and choices we want can be the most powerful way to live.

Finding your voice

The greatest feeling in the world will be when you say: "This is me, this is my voice. Listen to me because what I say has meaning and matters. I am not small, I am not big, I am just another person in this amazing world who seeks to feed myself and my family, and in doing so, make my difference."

This courage will happen in your life today, tomorrow or sometime in your future. You will know the moment when you know you matter, when you value yourself deeply, and know that the way others live their lives and run their businesses and share their 'perfect' version of themselves are all irrelevant to the life you seek and the whole person you are. You will see the dreams of others as empowering, not belittling. You will join in the celebration of those who win, because you will see yourself as a winner too.

Find your freedom

You may have felt silenced, you may have put up with people, situations and thoughts. But the moment you set yourself free of someone else's view of life and believe in your desires is the day you will throw your hands in the air and say: "Here I am. This is who I am and this is what I believe in, and this is what I am going to do about it." This is my personal manifesto.

Your personal manifesto – finding what deeply moves you

I have covered four of the five basic needs that Maslow wrote about in 1943. The one that shifts us the greatest and cannot happen without the previous four being met is what Maslow calls 'self actualisation'. "What a man can be, he must be" – this is a great quote that sums up this highest level. This level is the full potential for yourself.

Removing any over-ego, low self-worth, any limiting beliefs, anger, fear, defensiveness and being in control of the person you are and the life you want will take you closer to the full potential of yourself.

This does not happen from an intellectual perspective, but rather it creeps up on you. The power of it will thrill you, and from then on, your voice is formed. The full potential of why you were born will start to be revealed – first to you, and then to the world.

Be you – don't mimic others

I regularly observe a large group of people who have been on their only journey to peace and freedom. Their message to the world is without doubt a powerful message. The interpretation of the same self-help, self-development books that most enlightened people have read, crossed with their own life experiences and sometimes traumas, mean that if they can help one life then they have fulfilled a contribution on earth. The first life they helped was their own. This empathy and personal journey is the anchor for their teachings.

I also see these people using their strengths to an extreme, where their desire for success becomes an overdone one. They cannot stop marketing their greatness: sucked into the marketing engines and broadcasts of the modern age, they over-exaggerate their impact, over-share and over-shout about their greatness. The internet is full of these gurus and sadly some of them manipulate the lost souls that we can all be, with promises of eternal life – well perhaps not eternal life, but they promise them a lot!

Don't focus on what you lack

We have to be careful where we place our attention in this self-development world. Are we gaining skills and a mindset that empowers us, or is there an agenda that we can't always see? My take on this is that too many people focus on what they lack, rather than on what they already are. In saying you could be more successful, you buy into the fact you are not successful enough. In saying you could be richer, you believe you are not rich enough. In saying that you can be happier, you are not happy enough.

This type of marketing wants you to consider the gap between you and the world you could have. They focus on making you feel you lack something or need more. Watch out for this marketing trend and fight it in your head. We are so easily sold to. For instance, I was shocked to discover that it was a cereal brand in the early 20th century that told us all: "breakfast is the most important meal of the day". Think of this when you read marketing messages to stay in control of your own needs, because your needs are personal to you.

This book will have failed if you can't see that your version of life might already be what you wanted all along. Your version of success, wealth and happiness might actually be okay for you. Be brave enough to find the version of life that is yours and climb further up that mountain you have already been walking on.

Can we get back to the real promise of the connected world?

For me, the promise of the internet was one of deep connection, the reduction of loneliness and the joy of global kindness and friendship between business owners. The new social wave was not social at all. It was about who could shout, manipulate and win the most followers. No wonder it was really the birth of fake news, dopamine-driven systems that cause addiction, suicides, stress and depression in the young and the old.

Create your manifesto for your life

You can create your own manifesto. Is your dream to find your voice in business? Be brave and have the courage to stand up and make your difference – you are already on this path, your own personal mountain, your choice of summit, your choice of path and with the people you want to walk with.

These are amazing times, and when we bring our whole self into the whole world, we are truly free and able to use our own values, our own definition of success and our own awareness of what makes us happy. Don't allow the temptation of comparison to enter your life.

Go into the world as you and make your difference, small or large. Find your place and find your voice.

Finally, I want to thank you. The experience of writing this book and knowing that you would read it has helped me through the most difficult year of my life. We find ourselves in others and you have allowed me to truly find me.

I wish you love, and I wish you your success and your happiness. Find it, it is there, right inside you.

RESOURCES AND FURTHER SUPPORT

I have mentioned so many people and tools throughout the book. Rather than listing them all here, I have created a link of resources by chapter. These highlight TED Talks, experts, books, blogs and other helpful links relevant to each chapter. This is the most dynamic way I can keep you updated on the latest thoughts. There will be no requirement to sign in to gain access, so please feel free to click and enjoy.

www.pennypower.co.uk/resources

To get in touch with me

Facebook Group – Business is Personal
facebook.com/groups/pennyandthomas/

Instagram – pennyfpower

LinkedIn – www.linkedin.com/in/pennypower

My website – www.pennypower.co.uk

Twitter – @pennypower

Please do follow me on Twitter @pennypower and use the #businessispersonal hash tag so I can engage with you and send a picture of you holding my book so I can see you and follow you too.

I have a Twitter List called 'Business is Personal' where I follow the people that are relevant to the essence of my book, the experts and supporters of emotional and mental health. If you are one of these, please do tell me so I can add you to the list and also add your content to the Resources Section of my book, I am keeping this alive and adding all the time.

ABOUT THE AUTHOR

Penny Power OBE launched an online business community in 1998, four years before LinkedIn. Trailblazing this concept with her husband, Thomas Power, the two of them grew the network into a global community that supported hundreds of thousands of small businesses worldwide. In 2011, due to the banking crisis, Ecademy was sold and Penny began a personal journey of rebuilding her business and her life.

Penny has called herself an accidental entrepreneur for years and believes we need many emotional and mental tools to manage life as a business owner. Awarded an OBE by the Queen in January 2014 for the contribution Ecademy made, Penny has dedicated herself through her honest speaking, community building and friendship to thousands of business owners and corporate employees.

Penny is married to Thomas Power. She has three children, Hannah, Ross and TJ, and lives in the South of England. Penny places family as her highest value and extends that value into her business life.